"You Can't Ric Alaska. It's an island.

MT. MCKINLEY
NAT'L PARK
MT.
MCKINLEY   Fairbanks
                  North Pole
        DENALI
★ Anchorage   MT.
                         CAMPBELL
ALASKA   US
              CANADA   Dawson

Gulf of   YUKON
Alaska

                              NORTHWEST
                              TERRITORIES

                        MACKENZIE MOUNTAINS

Juneau   Watson
                    Lake
                   Mighty
                   Moe
         CANADA
         US
Stewart

        New
        Hazelton
        Smithers   ALBERTA

Pacific   Prince
Ocean   George

         BRITISH
         COLUMBIA   JASPER
                           NAT'L PARK

                    GLACIER   BANFF
                    NAT'L PARK   NAT'L PARK
Vancouver
                    KOOTENAY
                    NAT'L PARK

                              CANADA
                    GLACIER   UNITED STATES
WASHINGTON   NAT'L PARK
         ID
                         ● Missoula   MONTANA

Our travel path from Missoula, Montana to Anchorage, Alaska is shown here.
The solid line indicates paved roads. The dashed line indicates gravel roads.

"You Can't Ride a Bike to Alaska. It's an Island!"

Mickey Thomas

iUniverse, Inc.
New York Lincoln Shanghai

"You Can't Ride a Bike to Alaska. It's an Island!"

iUniverse books may be ordered through booksellers or by contacting:

iUniverse
2021 Pine Lake Road, Suite 100
Lincoln, NE 68512
www.iuniverse.com
1-800-Authors (1-800-288-4677)

ISBN-13: 978-0-595-37350-5 (pbk)
ISBN-13: 978-0-595-81747-4 (ebk)
ISBN-10: 0-595-37350-X (pbk)
ISBN-10: 0-595-81747-5 (ebk)

Printed in the United States of America

To: Will and Nelle

Contents

1

September 1980–June 1981

Sometime around the beginning of my second and last year of graduate school, in 1980, I was thumbing through a magazine a friend had given me that was published by an organization named Bikecentennial out of Missoula, Montana. Amidst the advertisements for bike components and entreaties for riding companions to exotic places, I happened across an article that described a bicycle trip five guys had made to Alaska the previous summer.

Now this seemed extraordinary to me. I had not spent a lot of time thinking of how one would get to Alaska, and it certainly never dawned on me that people could, or would ride a bicycle there. Alaska, to me, was one of those places you heard about in a faraway sort of way, mostly from history books or when the weatherman reported about impossibly cold temperatures in some mystical place such as Barrow or Nome. Because of that, I imagined it probably had two seasons, winter and Fourth of July. I always knew it was there, for sure, although I didn't really know anyone who had actually been there. In addition, it is difficult to find a map that will truly give Alaska its due. Alaska, of course, is not part of the contiguous forty-eight states, but is wholly connected to western Canada. Even so, United States maps often show Alaska not connected to Canada at all, but standing alone. Possibly because of space limitations on most maps we are not given a correct impression of Alaska's true size either.

With 591,004 square miles, Alaska is by far our largest state. Consider this: Alaska is twice as big as Texas, our second largest state, with 266, 807 square miles. It is almost forty-nine times larger than our smallest state, Rhode Island, which has 1,212 square miles. Alaska is the largest state area-wise, but it is the 48th of 50 states in population size. This equates to less than one person per square mile compared to Rhode Island with 865 people per square mile. It is so large that if you superimposed the state of Alaska across the lower forty-eight states, the eastern panhandle would start near Savannah, the western panhandle would end somewhere in western Mexico and in between Alaska would totally cover Kansas, Missouri, Illinois, Iowa, and Wisconsin. It would also partially cover the states of Georgia, Alabama, Tennessee, Kentucky, Arkansas, Nebraska, North and South Dakota, Minnesota, the Upper Peninsula of Michigan, Oklahoma, Texas, and New Mexico. I think you get a good idea of its immensity, now.

Of course, getting to Alaska by bicycle would also mean a rider would have to ride through the Canadian provinces of Alberta and British Columbia as well as the Yukon Territory. Alberta and British Columbia, combined, are roughly the same size as Alaska. Add in Yukon and you have some serious size and distance. A one-way trip from the cyclist's starting point in Missoula, Montana, to their stopping point in Anchorage, Alaska, would be about 3,400 miles, or about the distance between California and Virginia.

According to the article, the trip from Missoula to Anchorage took sixty-two days. Rain, sleet, or snow fell on forty-three of the days. Of the total distance of 3,400 miles, approximately 1,300 traveled were over gravel roads. The group averaged about seventy-four miles a day on pavement and about sixty miles a day on gravel. They ate the equivalent of fifteen pounds of peanut butter per man during the trip, but amazingly didn't lose or gain any weight. Lastly, it was a trip a bike mechanic would love. The group had thirty-one flats (twenty-six on gravel roads), they wore through sixteen tires, broke nineteen spokes, a hub, several rear axles (I didn't even know bikes had axles), and bent a rim.

Clearly, these guys were hardy, intrepid, and not very bright, but, oddly, I was attracted by the thought of making the same trip. I was drawn like a moth to a light.

I was not sure why, other than it seemed like a pretty good way to see parts of the U.S. and Canada that I'd only read about. It would enable me to unwind after two tough years of graduate study; I assumed it would get me in the best shape of my life; and finally, it would give me an experience to tell the grandchildren about. So, a little rashly, and in a fit of youthful testosterone, I decided to give it a try. And how hard could it be? I knew how to ride a bike already.

Predictably, my family and friends offered helpful encouragement. They said, "you'll never make it," and reminded me that the grizzlies would just be coming out of hibernation and would think a biker a tasty treat. More than one person looked at me with disbelief bordering on shock when I told them of my intentions. Most conversations went something like this:

"You're going where? On a what? Are you nuts? You'll never make it."

It all came to a rather goofy climax when a girl I knew laughed in my face after I told her about the trip. She sneeringly said, "You can't ride a bicycle to Alaska."

"Why not"?

"Because, Alaska's an island, doofus."

There were, of course, a few issues that had conveniently escaped me. I had a year-old bike that I wasn't sure could make the trip, I didn't have any bicycling or camping gear, and I had never even seen a loaded touring bicycle. Not to mention the fact that my bicycling experience had gotten off to a rather rocky start. As a little kid I couldn't start, stop, turn, or stay upright for more than a few seconds, even on flat ground. Out of timidity, I had kept my training wheels on much longer than my friends, and now I was behind them in biking skills.

My friend Phillip, already a good rider, was willing to help, and he decided it would be better for me to learn on his downward sloping backyard, reasoning that if you can't stay up on flat ground, then speed is what you need. This made perfect sense to my six-year old mind, and I took my training wheels off and pushed my bike to Phillip's house for my training session. Phillip's backyard was about eighty feet long, with one end about five feet lower than the other. It was a veritable obstacle course of bushes and toys, as well as his mother's clothesline.

Details are murky after all these years, but I have fleeting memories of my afternoon riding down Phillip's backyard that revolve around bouncing over toy car carriers, knifing through assorted shrubs and flower beds, and ending in spectacular crashes. The day finished abruptly with a rather unfortunate entanglement with Mrs. Rogers' clothesline and several of her freshly laundered foundation undergarments. I can still see the look of astonishment on her face as I hurtled past her kitchen window with assorted panties and brassieres flapping in the wind from my bike.

Now, with all these limitations blithely put behind me, I wrote Bikecentennial to sign on. In a couple of weeks or so, I received a letter of welcome, an itinerary, and an equipment list. In my eagerness and early non-planning, I hadn't anticipated all the effort it would take to get ready for the trip. I had been so clueless, it was impressive.

As I looked over the equipment list, the heading of "First Aid and Medicine" jumped out at me. I was startled to see a listing for Lomotil (for diarrhea), Noxzema (for chafing), and Preparation H (for hemorrhoid protection). This was almost a deal breaker for me. Number one, these ailments shouldn't happen to anyone under, say, seventy-five, and number two, I wasn't sure if anything could be more uncomfortable than riding long distances on a skinny bike seat, in the wilds of Canada and Alaska, while battling a bad case of chafed hemorrhoids and diarrhea.

Now that I was properly armed with an equipment list, I made an appointment with a guy named Rael at the local bike shop. Once there, I told him of my intention to ride a bicycle to Alaska, and he nodded with enthusiasm. Rael was one of those guys that had that agreeably shabby look of someone that had spent a lot of time in the great outdoors. Bearded, lanky to the point of being almost stringy, with a shock of blond hair, he was dressed in baggy shorts, a faded tee shirt, and Birkenstocks with socks. He was enthusiastic about my trip and obviously thought I had a lot more experience than I actually had.

"So, what kind of gearing will you be using?"

"Uh, gearing?" I said bewildered.

"Sure. Will you want 28 or 34 teeth on your rear cog?"

I feigned understanding and looked off reflectively.

"Didn't you say you were going to be spending several hundred miles on gravel roads?"

"Um, yes, I believe so."

"Well, I think you'll agree that 34 teeth would be best. You might need the 'granny gear' for all those hills."

I nodded and said, "Well, of course. Wouldn't everyone?"

"And you'll want center pull brakes instead of side pull brakes.

"Absolutely."

"Toe clips will help you ride more efficiently, too."

"Great! Gotta have efficient toes! Heh, heh."

He gave me a sideways glance, not knowing whether to take that as a joke.

His eyes narrowed and in a mild accusatory tone he said, "Didn't your list suggest installing fenders? A purist would never be caught dead with fenders."

I leaned forward and said in a mumble, "Well, the letter seemed to imply that there would be mud, you see."

"Do you want the panniers with the ripstop nylon or the panniers made in cordura?"

"What is your preference? Schraeder or Presta valves?"

And so it went for three hours.

Of course, everything was outrageously expensive. The panniers, which included front and rear bags and a handlebar bag, cost $224.26. The handlebar bag did come with a nifty see-thru map case that snapped onto the top of the bag. I liked this very much. I also bought a Bell helmet that resembled a shallow wash basin with a styrofoam interior.

It turned out that my bike was indeed trip-worthy after the addition of a new freewheel, some fine tuning on my spokes to make my wheels true, the addition of two very expensive front and rear racks to hold the front and rear panniers, and some new center pull brakes. (I had purchased a Kabuki/Bridgestone bike the year before mainly as transportation to and from graduate school with no obvious expectation of using it to take a trip to Alaska).

I bought two water bottles, a Zefal pump with a Schrader valve (I still was unclear what this was), two whole new tires, two tubes, a chain tool (to be able to remove the chain for cleaning), freewheel remover, spare spokes, pliers, spoke tightener, tire levers (for removing flattened tires), assorted nuts and bolts, WD 40 lubricant, and spare cable. The total cost to retrofit my bike for the trip: $743 and change. This was a little over $400 more than my bike cost brand new.

Rael gave me a cheery bon voyage and sent me on my way with the warning, "Watch out for the moose."

"The moose? Why?"

"Well, they're meaner than the bears."

I sputtered, "Meaner than grizzlies? How?"

"Bears will generally want to avoid you, a mad moose will seek you out and try and do bad things to you-especially if they are in rut."

I tried not to let my voice rise, "In a rut? Rael, are you saying a lovesick Yukon moose might confuse me for his prom date?"

"Nah, it'll probably never happen. I've only heard about a few times where that turned into a problem. Most of the people come out with only a few injuries."

"Most? Few?" My voice was really rising.

There were other people in the store and naturally they looked over to see what the ruckus was all about.

Rael looked about nervously and said, "Well, thanks again for coming, and good luck." And with that, I was out the door with visions of being stalked by an amorous moose.

The next day I continued my shopping at the camping store. What I needed mainly was a good lightweight tent, a sleeping bag, and rainwear. I kept reminding myself that I would be carrying everything and that extra pounds and ounces mattered. I found a North Face mummy sleeping bag that weighed 3.5 pounds and that was loaded with fiberfill reputed to stay warm even if wet and was effective down to about thirty-five degrees. I decided on a Timberline tent that weighed 7.5 pounds and was free standing, meaning it could stand alone without tent stakes. It could also be put up in about five minutes, which would be an important feature in the rain. Speaking of rain, I needed a rain jacket and rain pants. This was at a time when the fabric Gore-Tex was just becoming popular.

So I picked out a green rain jacket and a pair of mismatched green rain pants because the store didn't have any others. Even then, this was a very expensive purchase, but I decided I wanted to be a dry as possible. All this went pretty smoothly until Jill, the chipper salesperson, mentioned two more items she thought I needed. She brought out a section of rope and a small round bell like the jingle bells on a sleigh.

"I think you should carry this rope. It isn't too heavy and it would be perfect for hanging your food."

"Excuse me, did you say 'hanging my food'?"

"Sure, you don't want the bears rummaging through your tent at night looking for food, do you?"

"Um."

"You hang your food between two trees high enough that the bears can't reach it."

"Ah. Well what's the bell for? A dinner bell for the bears?"

"The bell is to let bears know you are coming. That way they'll hear you and will probably be gone by the time you get there. A surprised bear won't be a happy bear. Ha, ha, ha." She laughed at her own joke.

With an increasing sense of unease, I bought both.

I was beginning to feel like as if this trip was going to be memorable for all the wrong reasons.

2

June 1–June 5

I sent in my check to Bikecentennial and was now committed to riding a bicycle to Alaska. I felt like I was in pretty good physical shape. I jogged occasionally and I rode my bike to school every day and I intended to do more training during my last quarter of graduate school. But as the pressure of the last quarter started to build (I had to write a thesis, and pass oral and written exams), I neglected to do much in the way of anything other than study, write, and sleep. The panniers were still nicely boxed in the closet, as were the sleeping bag and tent. I did ride the equivalent of two eleven-mile rides in one day with Laura, a girl I was seeing. I was actually worn out from the twenty-two mile ride, and she was still going strong. She was from good Norwegian stock, and I was from Krispie Kreme stock. It was about this time that I started experiencing pain in both knees that a doctor diagnosed as tendonitis. This should have been a wake up call that there would be some serious consequences on the trip.

I fully expected to take the trip alone, but when Bikecentennial sent me the names of several others that had signed on, I figured it would be interesting to meet some new folks. We were supposed to meet in Missoula on June 4, to begin preparations for the trip.

Here is our group on the first day of the trip. From left to right: Garry, Arnold, Mickey, Henry, Dale, Tim, Pete, John, Tom and Steve.

Garry, one of the trip leaders, wrote that there were two guys in Wisconsin, Pete in Green Bay and Tim in Milwaukee, that had signed up for the trip and suggested we carpool together to save money. I called Pete and we decided I would drive my 1973 turd-brown Chevy Impala that I affectionately nicknamed Saphronia. Pete had built a makeshift bike rack (this was before high-tech racks) out of wood with attachments for the car. We would modify it to fit on top of my car after I arrived in Green Bay. I drove from my home in Tennessee and met Pete at a roadside stop in Chicago. Pete was about 35 years old, married with a son, and worked in the fledgling computer industry. He apparently was burned out from his work and had the blessings (though I thought with trepidations) from his wife. When we arrived in Green Bay we heard of another fellow that had decided at the last minute to join us on the ride. His name was John and he was madly trying to get his equipment together. I heard that he didn't even have a bike and went to the bike store and picked up everything the day before we left. John was nineteen years old, just out of high school, was about 5 '11 " and 160 pounds with curly blond hair and a kind of crooked smile. He was a beer-drinking, fun-loving sort with broad shoulders, a narrow waist, and the type of midwestern accent that pronounced Wisconsin as "Wiscaansin." He also was the type of personality that was able to see the positive in virtually everything. Like me, he had no bicycle touring experience.

Miraculously, John was able to get everything together in time for our departure from Green Bay. Pete, John, and I drove from Green Bay to Milwaukee to pick up Tim at his apartment. Tim had been on a cross-country bicycle tour a year or so before and had been saving money from his factory job for this trip since then. He was about 5 '9 " and 200 pounds, with long, blond hair and wire-rimmed glasses. He was very quiet and rarely said anything unless one of us asked him a direct question. He also turned out to be a deceptively strong rider.

Together, we headed northwest in Saphronia. We traveled all day across Wisconsin and the next through Minnesota and North Dakota. We crossed into Montana with a leaky fuel pump that was sucking gas alarmingly. A couple of hours in a Miles City garage and fifty dollars later had us back on the road for the rest of the trip across Montana. We hit Missoula in the very late afternoon and checked into the Birchwood youth hostel, which was where our group would be staying until departure day.

The Birchwood was a long, wood-frame building painted a kind of sea-foam green. It had a common area living room with old, but comfortable mismatched furniture, a sparse kitchen, and a large, coed bunkroom with about fifteen bunk beds. There were separate bathrooms for men and women, but was offset by people parading back from the shower, in various states of undress, to the coed bunk-room. This didn't seem to bother anyone. The people populating the Birchwood were mainly travel-savvy young people heading to other parts of the west on sightseeing trips or were riding bicycles across the country on the Bikecentennial bike trail, which goes from Astoria, Oregon, passes through Missoula, and ends in Yorktown, Virginia. Virtually everyone had been traveling for extended periods and looked like it. The men mostly wore scraggly beards and had shaggy hair. Both men and women had worn looking clothes. Backpacks or panniers littered the floor. The majority were Americans with a sprinkling of foreign tourists, mainly from Germany. The thing that I found intriguing was that everyone, and I mean everyone, was friendly and cheerful. They also had that clear-eyed look of good health and discovery. In the midst of all this youthful exuberance was one older gentleman who looked as fit and wide-eyed as the younger group. His name was Henry and was a sixty-three year old from Pennsylvania. He was gentle, slightly built, about 5 ' 6 " and a sinewy 130 pounds, balding with a gray beard, and he had shiny bright blue eyes. He had an almost mystical quality about him, like the Dalai Lama, and he was regaling a small but admiring group about his plan to be on the Alaska bike ride. I eased into the circle of people in time to hear that he had slept outside in his tent every night during the Pennsylvania winter to prepare himself for the trip. He had also ridden his bicycle across the country several years before and had taken many training rides through the hills of Pennsylvania with his panniers loaded.

"Uh, oh," I thought to myself. I had only ridden a total (maybe) of one hundred or so miles as practice, and hadn't yet slept in my tent and my sleeping bag, or loaded my panniers. I had put up the tent for practice once, and had even applied waterproof seam sealer so rain wouldn't seep through the stitching of the seams. As I looked around the room I suddenly felt soft and cushy like the fluffy pillows on your grandmother's couch. In fact, I stuck out like a sore thumb amongst all the grizzled travelers staying at the Birchwood. I was a cream puff....

I found an unoccupied top bunk and claimed it for the next two nights. At about this time several other people on the Alaska trip showed up. Garry, the leader, and Dale, the co-leader, introduced themselves and introduced us to Tom, Steve, and Arnold. Including Henry, there would be ten of us on the trip. Tom, about 30, was from Albuquerque, and was tall, bespectacled, recently divorced, and blessed with a wry sense of humor. Steve was from Dallas, aged 26, with longish brown hair and a good start on a beard. Arnold, about 26, had ridden his bike to meet us and already had that disheveled road look; and he had many bike tours to his credit. He was also from Pennsylvania, and we discovered he would be carrying a lot of medicine with him because he had had a kidney transplant several years before. Garry, 32, most recently living in Seattle, was a former school teacher, had led several bicycling tours, and had also led the group of five guys on the Alaska trip that I had read about in the Bikecentennial magazine. He was quiet, introspective, direct and to the point, and had a dry sense of humor. Dale, the co-leader had several cross-country bike tours under his belt and had worked the previous winter as a cross-country ski instructor for the Von Trapp family at their ski lodge in Stowe, Vermont. He was an engineer by training, and had a bubbly sense of humor. He also looked to be in the best shape of all of us.

The next day was spent riding around Missoula to various bike shops to round up last minute items. We also spent some time being interviewed by the Missoula paper, which was interested in our trip because we were the largest group at the time to ever embark on a trip to Alaska by bicycle. They asked why we were interested in such a long and difficult trip. We were very clever with our answers, "We have nothing better to do," or "Because it's there." When I was asked how I paid for the trip, I jokingly answered that I sold my piano. The reporter took that comment for gospel and dutifully put in the paper as fact. I didn't own a piano.

Good group dynamics are important for a trip like this. Individuals from many different economic and educational backgrounds are joined together and have to learn to work, ride, socialize, and resolve differences together. On this trip, we would be carrying everything ourselves (food, clothing, equipment), and would share the cooking and shopping duties. It was essential that everyone get along. No one was exempt from group duties, and each needed to pull his own weight.

The night before the trip I started to get butterflies in my stomach like I did before participating in a track meet or football game. I was beginning to wonder if I was way out of my league in attempting this ride. The majority of guys signed on for the trip were veteran cyclists. Several (Arnold, Garry, Dale, Henry, and Tim) had all ridden across the United States. All of the others (except John, who had decided at the last minute to join the trip) had wisely spent a lot of time training for the trip and were comfortable with the distances required. The next day was going to be the first day I had ridden a fully loaded touring bicycle. Now, I wasn't even sure about what to pack or even how to pack my bags. The big panniers now seemed impossibly small as I tried to figure out what to take and where to pack it.

The others were helpful but were spending their own time packing and getting ready, so I was largely on my own about what to take. Garry told me to try and concentrate most of the heavier items low in the panniers and in the rear bags. The front bags should be lighter. Garry handed each one of us five large garbage bags. I wasn't sure what they were for, and he said, "Put one into each of your panniers and one into your stuff sack for your sleeping bag. They will help keep your clothes and sleeping bag dry."

I naively said, "I bought waterproof panniers, and my sleeping bag stuff sack is waterproof, too."

Garry gave me a look that shouted, "You rookie!" but he recovered his deference and said, "Well, the manufacturers all say their stuff is 'waterproof,' but it really isn't. They probably charge extra for saying it is waterproof, though."

"Oh, uh, great; thanks for the bags."

And I stuffed my panniers and stuff sack with garbage bags and began the task of trying to put all my worldly belongings for the next ten weeks into four bags the size of large briefcases and a handlebar bag the size of a medium sized purse.

Into the rear panniers, I put an extra pair of running shoes (I would be riding in running shoes, too), four pairs of underwear, four tee-shirts, three pairs of white socks, three pairs of nylon shorts, a long sleeved blue and white striped button down shirt, a long sleeved red checkered wool shirt, an orange Tennessee football jersey, a polyester tennis warm-up jacket, a pair of blue-jeans, two pairs of wool socks, and toiletries (no razor!). In the front panniers, I put my Gore-Tex rain pants and rain jacket, various tools, a couple of paperback books *Zen and the Art of Motorcycle Maintenance* and *Night of the Grizzlies*. In my handlebar bag I put some more tools, some maps of the early part of the trip, a Nikon 35 millimeter camera, wool gloves, my wallet with travelers checks, and the next day's lunch of a peanut-butter sandwich and cookies. Unloaded, my bike weighed about 30 pounds. Fully loaded the bike weighed about 80 pounds. The most useless thing I would take was a flashlight. I didn't realize that the farther north we went, the longer the sun stayed up, so that when we finally arrived in Alaska the sun was out for about 20 hours a day and was only a kind of twilight during the time it was "night."

Several of us were running on adrenalin and stayed up talking. There were the usual nervous conversations about whether such and such was going to make the whole trip, or whether so and so would be a pain in the backside. But mostly we reflected on the coming ride. And so, with a little over 100 miles of training, I was about to spend the next ten weeks attempting to ride nearly 3,400 miles. We were to pass through two states (Montana and Alaska), two Canadian provinces (Alberta and British Columbia), one territory (Yukon), five National Parks (Glacier/Waterton in Montana, Kootenai in British Columbia, Banff and Jasper in

Alberta, and Denali in Alaska), spend approximately a month on gravel roads, cross the continental divide seven times, and ride into the last great wilderness in North America where bears and moose outnumber people. I finally went to bed and slept fitfully.

3

June 5–June 6

✦

107 miles from Missoula

June 5, 1981, dawned bright and sunny. Our group finished last-minute packing and assembled for the obligatory beginning-of-the-trip picture in front of the Birchwood. Our plan was to start around 8:30am and ride for a hearty western breakfast at the locally famous Old Town Café, which had a reputation of giving extra generous portions to bikers. It was something of a tradition for bikers leaving Missoula on whatever trips to stop for breakfast at the Old Town. As we left the Birchwood and headed for the Old Town Café, I climbed aboard and started to ride my fully loaded bike for the first time. Oh my gosh, I was shocked at how heavy and sluggish it felt. It was almost like having driven a sports car and then switching to a tractor trailer. Or a tank. It took longer to get started and longer to stop, and I could see there was going to be a steep learning curve for me during the next few days.

It was easy to see why bikers liked the Old Town Café, our servings came on platter sized plates and the single portions of eggs, hash browns, bacon, and toast would have made two regular sized meals for most anybody except hungry bikers.

After we gorged ourselves, we waddled out to our bikes, our stomachs full of food and ready to go. Missoula is a small, clean city. Even so, we had gone only a block or so when Arnold got a flat tire after he ran over some glass at a street corner. We were riding as a group at this point and in a show of support we all stayed with Arnold until his tire was repaired. This put us back a few minutes, but soon we were on our way out of town and riding through Hells Gate Canyon on Route 200. The road followed Camas Creek along which we had lunch, and went through some beautiful mountain valleys. That's what the map said; I was bent over my handlebars huffing and puffing. We made the turn north on Route 83 at Clearwater Junction towards our first stop, Seeley Lake. As soon as we made the turn the road began to rise into a gradual eight-mile hill. I was not used to shifting gears for the loaded bike and my chain came off three times before it was fixed with a minor adjustment. It was also here that I started to realize I had two other problems: my knees were starting to get stiff and, more alarmingly, I was getting numb in my groin area. Pete, who rode alongside me, just laughed when I told him about getting numb. I didn't think this was the least bit funny, but he explained that I should lower the front of my seat and the problem would resolve itself. A few more adjustments fixed the seat problem, and I hoped it would fix the numbness as well.

I could tell my knees were going to be a problem going forward. I would get occasional shooting pains through them that would almost take my breath away. Dale had told me that it was much more efficient to stay seated while riding up hills. This was something I had never done before, always preferring to stand up and pedal up hills. It turned out that riding up hills in a seated position was not the right solution for me, but that wouldn't become apparent to me until about three days later. The eight-mile hill seemed to go on forever, and I was reminded of my first day in the first grade when it seemed like the day would never end. We were only fifty or so miles into the ride. If I was falling apart now, how could I keep this up another 10 weeks?

We arrived, after fifty-six miles, at Seeley Lake and set up camp at a beautiful campsite next to the lake. The group did pretty well on the first day's ride, although all of us were tired and stiff. I was exhausted. My knee felt loose. I don't know how to explain that other than to say that it felt like a train had come off its tracks inside my right knee. Dale suggested a swim in Seeley Lake as a way to unwind from the ride while Garry and Tim cooked a dinner of vegetables, omelets, milk, and bread for the group.

The water of Seeley Lake was FREEZING! I mean, we are talking just short of ice floating in the water cold. Naïve, I had been coaxed to jump off of the dock first, had come up sputtering from the shock of the cold water, and was now trying to run across the top of the water to shore. I was over the localized numbness of the afternoon only to be numb from head to toe now.

I had never been in water this cold, not even on a canoe or raft trip. Naturally, early June in Montana logically means that there will be creeks and streams loaded with runoff from the snowfields in the mountains. Somehow this was lost on me. Everyone else gingerly got into the water while I hurriedly swam to shore invigorated enough for the next three days. Dale leisurely swam around the lake seemingly unaffected by the cold. He had spent the winter in Vermont teaching cross-country skiing for the Von Trapp family, so I imagined that he swam in frozen ponds.

Garry had mapped out our approximate route and mileages during the trip the year before, and we had a pretty good idea how far we were to ride each day as well as where we were planning to stay. We would mostly stay in campgrounds or rest areas, with occasional stays at local community centers or churches when the weather was bad or whenever we wanted a change. Two guys would alternate cooking two days so that every ten days or so each person was responsible for shopping and cooking for the group. Lunches were generally going to be sandwiches made from generous amounts of peanut butter, jam, honey, or anything else we were willing to add to it.

I had been standing next to John on the first day as he opened the Saran Wrap holding his sandwich.

"Ewww, what's that smell?" I said.

"Oh, it's a sardine, onion and cheese sandwich."

"John, that's nasty!"

"Well, I don't like peanut butter. So, I'll eat this instead."

I made a mental note: Don't ride behind John immediately after lunch....

There were ten of us and we could either ride as a large group, in small groups, or individually. It was made clear, however, that if anyone wanted dinner he needed to be at the stopping point by about 6:00 PM.

We had been lucky with a day of sunshine on the first day, but it rained in sheets during the night and we woke up to a cold drizzle that turned into a steady rain after lunch. When we hit Swan Lake after fifty-one miles we were all pretty wet and miserable. Garry was able to arrange for us to stay at the Swan Lake Community Center, an old wooden building with one large room, a kitchen, and two bathrooms. Finding free indoor lodging for ten wasn't easy, but it was a gift that Garry had that became even more apparent and welcome during the trip. The community center had two things going for it: it was warm and dry. A frustrating aspect of the day's ride was that while we were getting rained on, a nearby mountain range that was visible for most of the day appeared to be bathed in warm sunshine. Another frustration was that two days of riding was taking its toll on my knees. They were starting to hurt more and the ache was taking longer to subside. My knees were starting to swell, so I took a walk with Henry after dinner to loosen them up, and I found out that he had joined a sky diving club at age fifty. He has done so much with his life, and said that he wouldn't be sorry if he died that day.

4

June 7–9

◆

269 miles from Missoula

Steve and Henry cooking dinner in
the rain at Glacier National Park.

It was the third day of the trip, and I was homesick. We started riding in bright sunshine that turned to rain after about thirty miles. We camped in Apgar, after sixty-two miles, next to Lake McDonald, not far from West Glacier, Montana, and the weather was about forty degrees and raining. All our spirits were running low, so we decided to eat pizza in town to raise morale. The pizza restaurant was closed, so we went back to the campground to cook and eat dinner outside in the elements. We huddled into small, disconsolate groups and ate runny food in the cold rain. The weather was downright gloomy, and it was taking a toll on everyone, especially me. I had never been so far away from home before, and I missed my family and friends terribly. I knew that it was probably sunny and warm at home as opposed to cold and rainy in West Glacier. I was also getting frustrated with my sore knees, and this was adding to my melancholy. Climbing into my tent early

16

to get out of the rain, and having nothing much to do other than to worry about my knees, really increased the homesickness, too.

We were only a few days into the trip, and I was trying to keep an open mind about the ride. But I was not enjoying the weather and found my thoughts being drawn back home. I began to see the trip as more than just a physical challenge but also one that was going to be an even greater mental challenge. I expected that I would become used (assuming my knees would hold up) to riding long distances in the coming weeks. I also expected that it would be harder mentally to wake up every morning knowing that there were going to be a lot of miles to ride that day, in all sorts of weather and road conditions.

I was actually glad to be in Glacier National Park. I had heard and read about the park for a number of years and had been looking forward to seeing it. It is a park of almost unbelievable majesty and grandeur. Glaciers carved great valleys and lakes during the last ice age. It has more varieties of plants and wildlife than anyplace except the Great Smoky Mountains. The mountains rise into great jagged peaks that form the continental divide. It has one of the largest populations of grizzly bears in the lower forty-eight states and more permanent snowfields than anywhere in the continental U.S., other than Mount Rainier, Washington.

Glacier National Park became the country's tenth national park in 1910 after George Bird Grinnell, an early explorer to this part of Montana, spent many years getting the park established. Archaeological surveys found that humans had inhabited the area for over 10,000 years, and were probably the ancestors of tribes that still live in the area now. The Blackfeet Indians controlled the vast prairie lands east of the mountains while the Kootenai and Salish Indians lived and hunted the western mountain valleys long before the first European explorers arrived. The entire area was and is considered of great spiritual importance by all three tribes.

In the early 1800's the Lewis and Clark expedition came very near Glacier and soon thereafter trappers and settlers began steadily moving into the area forcing the Blackfeet, Salish, and Kootenai Indians onto reservations east and southwest of Glacier respectively. In 1891, the railroad over Marias Pass, southeast of Glacier, was completed allowing more settlers to populate the area. The mountains east of the continental divide were acquired in 1895 from the Blackfeet under pressure from miners looking for gold and copper. No large gold or copper deposits were discovered and the mining boom went bust after a few years.

Around the turn of the century, entrepreneurs starting looking at Glacier differently. They recognized the value of Glacier's spectacular scenic beauty. Facilities for tourists started springing up around West Glacier, where visitors could get off the train, take a stagecoach ride to Lake McDonald, and then board a boat for an eight-mile voyage to the Snyder Hotel. At this point, there were no roads into the wilderness and travel was better conducted by boat. Through the efforts of Mr. Grinnell and others, Glacier was opened as a forest preserve until it officially became a national park with the signature of President Taft.

Because of the creation of the park and the growing numbers of visitors, facilities were constructed to house park rangers and staff to protect the park. Roads, trails, and hotels were constructed and, in addition, the Great Northern Railway built backcountry chalets. Typically, guests would ride the train to the park, take a multi-day horseback trip visiting different hotels or chalets. The lack of roads meant the Glacier was accessible only to the hardiest of travelers. Eventually, it became clear that a road across the mountains was needed to accommodate less hardy travelers wanting to experience Glacier's increasingly famous scenery. This perception led to the construction of Going-to-the-Sun Highway.

The construction of Going-to-the-Sun Highway was a major undertaking that is still a marvel to today's visitors. It took over eleven years of work to complete the road, with the final section over Logan Pass being completed in 1932. Because the road is such an engineering feat, it is listed as a National Historic Landmark and is one of the most scenic roads to be found anywhere in North America. It is the only road that crosses the park, and it crosses the continental divide (the line at which water runs either east toward the Atlantic Ocean or west towards the Pacific) at Logan Pass, the highest point of the road at 6,680 feet.

Crossing this road from the southwest side of the park to the northeast side was our main goal for the fourth day of the trip, one that had been occupying our thoughts ever since we were in Missoula finishing preparations for the trip. Garry told us that the ride over Going-to-the-Sun Highway was considered one of the hardest and most amazing bike rides in the United States and that we should be "fired up." It would be comparable to some rides in the Tour de France that traverse the Alps, except that we would have the added honor of doing the ride on a loaded touring bike. We could expect to see lots of animals, tourists, and snow, since the road had been open only for a few days after its normal winter closure because of snow.

Garry told us that the road was relatively flat for several miles and that as it started upward towards the pass, it would become narrow and steep. Then, as a way to make the ride sink in, he said that after the steep part, the last eight miles would be more difficult. In fact, it was about a thirty-mile uphill climb from Apgar. The road, he said, was well maintained, but mostly two lanes. It was cut from the side of the mountain and appeared to hang out over the glacial valleys separated only by a small rock wall about three feet high. He told us that tourists and their RV's could be especially dangerous since the road was narrow, they would likely be watching the scenery instead of looking out for bikers, and we would be riding on the side of the road closest to the low wall separating us from a huge drop off and biker oblivion.

Going To The Sun Highway in Glacier National Park.
We had just ridden up the road next to the river.

This last little warning really did wonders for jump-starting my adrenalin flow for the day. Imagine Bert and Imogene from Wauwatosa, out on a tour of the west in their newly purchased, too-big-for-the-Going-to-the-Sun Highway RV, looking at the gorgeous scenery, feeling a slight bump that was a biker, now airborne like Wile E. Coyote, only to disappear as a little puff of dust at the end of a 1,000-foot drop. Bert and Imogene would continue on their merry way while the biker would become petrified and would be found, still gripping his handlebars, by archeologists 2,000 years later.

Garry said that once we crossed Logan Pass it would be mostly downhill to our next stopping point just outside of St.Mary/Babb, which is where the prairie meets the mountains.

It was the fourth day out of Missoula, and we were ready for this ride. We had heard about it and had been thinking about it for several days, and we all felt like someone does before a big game. All the pre-game hype was over. It was Ohio State vs. Michigan, Tennessee vs. Alabama, and Southern Cal vs. Notre Dame all wrapped into one. Now it was time to play and we wanted to get started.

It had rained all night again. There were low clouds, fog, drizzle, and it was about forty-five degrees when I hit the road. I was so psyched, that I left about forty-five minutes before everyone else. The road went alongside Lake McDonald for a ways, then passed through a low-lying, swampy area, where I saw my first moose standing knee deep in the water unconcernedly watching me ride by while it munched a breakfast of tender water plants.

I pedaled upwards through valleys carved by glaciers at the end of the last ice age. The road sliced through forests of evergreen trees, like cedars and hemlocks, and crossed over rushing streams of water from the snow melt. It rained harder just as I passed through a tunnel carved from the rock. The road did a switchback and headed into the clouds. Below, I could see the lush green valley I had just ridden through. Its sides had been rounded by the glaciers so that the valley resembled a great long U. McDonald Creek, which I had followed for several miles, was visible as a silver thread winding towards Lake McDonald.

The conditions, however, had gotten even worse; the temperature was dropping and the tourist traffic was increasing. I had left Apgar early enough to beat the rush but now the traffic had caught up to me. I had finished the first twenty-two miles in a relatively comfortable two and a half hours but I was starting to feel the strain and fatigue of the three previous days of riding fifty-six, fifty-one, and sixty-two miles respectively. There were still eight more miles to the top of the pass, and I could see the road climbing into the clouds.

This was more than I could take, and all of a sudden I hit the figurative "wall." The gorilla jumped on my back. I couldn't go anywhere. I was in a mental fog. I pulled off the road onto a small parking area at an overlook to try and get myself together. My knees felt as if someone were sticking knives into them, and then maliciously twisting the handle. With every crank of my pedals bursts of light went off in my head like flashbulbs. My thigh muscles felt as if they were going to spontaneously combust. I could feel every little sinew pinging with pain. Oddly, my shoulders were hurting from gripping the handlebars as the road got steeper. I was wet on the outside from the rain and underneath my clothing I was wet from the sweat. And, I had drunk all the water in both water bottles miles ago and was now resorting to filling them with runoff from the cliff walls next to the road. I was exhausted. I had never felt so tired or as discouraged knowing the hardest part of the ride was still ahead.

An RV pulled into the overlook parking lot and splashed me with slush from the road. I could see an older man and woman consulting a guidebook and squinting through the fogged up window to try and make out the scenery. When they saw me they climbed out of the RV and ambled toward me in a friendly way.

I was in absolutely no mood to be amiable and was trying to summon my courage to get back on the road when the man spoke up.

"How far are you going on that bike, son?"

"Anchorage, Alaska," I wearily replied. He looked stunned.

"You're riding where?" He looked as if he were questioning my sanity (At this point, I had real concerns about my sanity, too!).

"Honey, come here, ya gotta meet this fella. He says he's riding his bicycle all the way to Anchorage, Alaska. Can you believe that? How many miles is that, young fella?"

I didn't really want to continue this conversation.

"About thirty-three hundred more miles from here, I guess."

He let out an appreciative "hoo whee" and his wife sucked in a long reflective breath as they shivered in the wind and rain.

"Hon, don't we know somebody that rode their bike somewhere?"

His wife helpfully chimed in, "You know, you're right. Didn't Pat's nephew ride his bike to, to,…oh, I forget where?"

"No, no" said the man, "it wasn't Pat's nephew was it? It was…it was…well, anyway, we know someone that rode his bike, too."

The wind picked up and the rain was turning to sleet.

"That's great!" I said, not really caring. "Have a good trip." I turned to head back to the road.

The lady said in a grandmotherly tone, "You look awfully cold. We were just going to stop here for a bite to eat. How would you like warm yourself in the RV while I fix you a sandwich and a nice cup of hot chocolate?"

Halleluiah, the Angels were singing!

There was world peace!

The stock market was in a perpetual bull market!

It was my turn to be stunned.

I said, "Um, sure, I mean, only if I'm not intruding…."

The lady said, "Don't be silly. Come in and get warm. You can finish your ride to wherever, later."

Their names were Dot and Sam, and they were from Sioux Falls, not Wauwatosa. They were headed to Waterton, and I was jealous to realize it would take them about three hours of driving what would take me two more days of riding.

On the way out they splashed me again, but I didn't mind, and I was in much better humor to finish the last few miles to the top.

It took another three hours to ride the last eight miles to the top of Logan Pass. My knees continued to make my eyes tear up and I was drinking water at an amazing rate considering how cold and wet it was. Luckily, there was plenty of cliff runoff.

I was like a tourist magnet every time I stopped for a breather. Thanks to Dot and Sam from Sioux Falls, I was in a much better frame of mind to answer the inevitable questions. Teens and little kids ran through the rain and sleet to ask me where I was going and how far I was riding, and then they would hustle back to their warm cars while I plodded along upward.

I finally reached the top in a freezing rain and waited as Pete, Arnold, and John pulled in right behind me. All of us had struggled to the top and were exhausted. Arnold had brought a ceremonial bottle of Champaign to celebrate the ride up to the pass. He passed it around to everyone present for a drink, and even though I don't drink, I took a small sip. John took a really big sip, a swig really, and so did Pete. When it came around to me again, I declined, and the bottle was expertly emptied by the others.

The temperature was 34 F and I was not inclined to stay around waiting for the others to show up. Besides, it was almost snowing and the pass was snow-bound except for the plowed road and parking lot at the rest room. As I filled my water bottles in the rest room sink it occurred to me that I had averaged about 2.6 miles an hour over the last eight miles and that I had drunk six full bottles of water during that time, or the equivalent of 1.3 pint bottles of water per mile!

Garry told us that the ride down the other side would make the ride up worth it. I was all for getting some free miles out of the way by going downhill. What was not expected was that it would be so cold on the way down that I would have to stop several times to shake my hands to get feeling back in them. The temperature was in the forties on the way down the other side. Add in the wind chill and the fact that I was wet, and it made it piercingly cold. It was, however, a glorious ride down (it took twenty-five minutes!), and when I got to St. Mary, on the eastern side of the park, after fifty-eight miles, it was about 60 degrees and sunny. It was unbelievable how much difference a few miles made in the weather. And very welcome.

That night, Tim and I cooked the group meal: a soup with lentils, carrots, onions, green beans and potatoes. Not bad for the first attempt. The wind howled all night through the grove of trees where we camped, it sounded like a freight train running through my tent. My bike blew over several times and I was slightly concerned during the night that my tent would roll end over end into Lower St. Mary's Lake with me in it. It was like trying to sleep in a wind tunnel.

The next morning was sunny and cool, and everyone was eager for the days ride-everyone except me. I had blown my wad on the ride up Going-to-the-Sun Highway, and I had nothing left. I was running on fumes. My knees were worse than ever and I could barely walk or bend down to take my tent down. Garry and

Dale both were sympathetic and suggested I ride only in the lowest gears of my bicycle and go slow. We were to ride forty-two miles to the town of Waterton in Alberta, Canada, where we would take our first rest day (we generally took one rest day a week).

I started out early and was soon passed by everyone (even 63-year-old Henry, who was usually the last rider, passed me like I was going backwards!). On flat ground, in a low gear, I was relatively pain free. Downhills were easy; uphills were another story. I had to get off my bike and push up every dadgummed hill. I'm sure that out of forty-two miles that day, I walked at least fifteen. Several of the guys rode with me at different times during the day to help keep my spirits up while I was bike-walking. We stopped several times during the day to rest and snack. On one particularly glorious occasion the sun was warm and we were sitting in a field of wild flowers looking at the imposing block of 9,000 foot Chief Indian Mountain. It was here that I learned, however, that at least two of the guys, Tom and Pete, were wavering on whether to continue the trip. Tom was just completing a divorce, and I assumed he came on this trip to try to clear his head after the previous year or so. Pete was missing his wife and son in Green Bay. I hated to think they would leave the trip after such a short time and hoped they would grit it out for the duration. I had to admit, though, that I had been wavering in my commitment, too. I hadn't expected almost debilitating knee problems, and I was not too enthused about riding in more bad weather for what seemed like an inordinate amount of time. But I did have one thing that made me want to grind it out. My cousin Bill, who I greatly respect, told me before the trip that I wouldn't be able to make it. I had to prove him wrong.

5

June 9–11

◆

342 miles from Missoula

Waterton Lakes National Park was founded in 1895, and it is where some of the oldest mountains in the Rockies rise abruptly from the prairies of western Alberta. The park adjoins Glacier National Park to form Waterton-Glacier International Peace Park. It is a land forged from fire, flooding, and wind. Jagged mountains rise almost vertically from the turquoise waters of Upper Waterton Lake. Wind is nearly constant, blowing through the Waterton Valley as it brings weather that is changeable by the minute. It would rain, hard for several minutes, and then turn to warm sunshine for several minutes, and then rain again on this cycle during our stay there. The historic and rustically elegant Prince of Wales Hotel sits high on a peninsula of land that juts into Upper Waterton Lake. The hotel, opened in 1927, has survived fires, floods, and the twin financial calamities of the depression and World War II. Bighorn sheep wander from the nearby mountains and graze on the grass outside the hotel.

We had passed through the Canadian/U.S. border without any problems (it had a fabulous four mile downhill into Waterton), and we cruised into town around 5:00 PM. We quickly set up our tents in the town campground on the shores of Upper Waterton Lake and settled in for a much needed couple of rest days to mend our aches and bruised psyches.

I slept late and spent the morning writing letters and penning the first of what I hoped would be several articles on the progress of the trip in my hometown newspaper. It was also necessary to do laundry for the first time and to enjoy the first hot shower since we left Missoula five days before. I had taken a frigid swim in Seely Lake and had endured a less than lukewarm shower at the campground in St.Mary/Babb, so I had extra appreciation for the hot-water making capabilities at our little campground in Waterton.

Later, Garry and Dale both noticed how gingerly I was moving about and how I was favoring my knees.

Garry said, "You look like you're miserable, and I would guess you have tendonitis in your knees. If you do have tendonitis, it won't go away unless you rest your knees. You need to understand what your options are."

I wasn't sure where this was leading. Maybe they would arrange to set up a ride for me. Say, on a van on a bus?

"Okay," I said, "What are my options?"

Garry leaned forward and in a quiet tone said, "You can continue riding your bike or you can hitchhike until your knees feel better."

Incredulous I sputtered, "That's it? Those are my options?"

"Pretty much." Dale said. "Whatever you choose, you'll need to get to the next stopping point by dinner, or else you'll need to be responsible for where you eat and stay. The group needs to keep moving."

"So, the group would just continue on while I would be responsible for staying within reach?"

"Yep." Dale said. Garry nodded.

I pondered the sobering thought of trying to ride through the pain of knees ravaged by tendonitis, or of trying the unwieldy feat of hitching a ride, while out in the middle of nowhere, with strangers willing to pick up a bulky bicycle and its smelly rider. Neither option looked very promising. I'm sure arranging a van or bus never occurred to either of them and would probably go against some unwritten rule of making the experience too easy.

"Uh, okay, I'll try to ride, and if that doesn't work, I'll try to hitch a ride." The next several days are going to be very interesting, I thought, as I hobbled off to my tent.

The next day dawned warm and crystal clear. I decided that it would be a good thing to wear my blue jeans all day in an attempt to keep my knees warm. We ate breakfast and everyone packed up and left at his own pace. I started out strong but struggled up the hill out of Waterton so much that I had to push my bike the rest of the way to the main road. Once there, the road looked reasonably flat to rolling. The prairie was to my right and the mountains were to my left. There was a very strong wind coming off the prairie that shifted into a headwind as the road turned into it. I was now totally alone for the first time on the trip. Except for the ride over Going to the Sun Highway, I had ridden with at least two or more of the guys. The group had all ridden ahead and I was left to my own devices. The headwind was making riding in lower, easier gears seem like I was riding in higher gears and it was not long before the familiar shooting pain in my knees returned. Here I was, alone, out on the edge of the prairie in southwestern Alberta with dwindling options. Riding would be impossible if I wanted to catch the group. It now came to trying my luck at hitching a ride.

How *does* one hitch a ride? I had never hitched a ride before and had seen only what looked like vagrants trying to hitch rides back in the States. Plus, I had always heard never to pick up a hitchhiker for fear that he would be an axe murderer recently escaped from the state penitentiary. I had heard gruesome stories of unsuspecting and well-meaning people with axes cleaving their newly dead head . And now, would people drive by and eye me with the same suspicion I was taught to have?

And what about people that picked up hitchhikers? I supposed there were people that would get their jollies by picking up hitchhikers, bashing them in the head, and then disposing of them in some unmarked shallow grave.

I was really uneasy, but seeing no other way, I stuck out my thumb and tried to look reputable.

Several cars whizzed by and several more even slowed down before they sped back up. I was having no luck. I started walking with my thumb out while I pushed my bike with the other and in no time a van stopped and asked if he could give me a lift. At first glance the guy seemed nice enough as he helped me put my bike in the back all the while asking friendly questions about my trip: if I was hitching because of a flat tire, where I was riding, where I was from. Maybe axe murderers softened up their victims with small talk. I warily got into the passenger seat trying to appear like a guy not to be messed with. If he asked, my name would be "Butch."

His name was Jim and was headed to Pincher Creek, about twenty or so miles up the road, to buy a replacement part for a broken tractor. He wouldn't let me pay him for gas and dropped me off with a cheery "good luck, eh" (Western Canadians have this agreeable way of finishing their sentences with "eh"). Well, my first experience at hitchhiking had been successful enough; I had twenty miles behind me on what would be a seventy-two plus mile day of riding and I didn't have a new part in my hair from an axe.

At Pincher Creek, the road turned west, and I continued to push my bike with my thumb out. Within about thirty minutes, a truck passed me, pulled off the road about 100 yards ahead and started backing towards me. As the truck came to a stop, I saw there were two girls in their late teens in it. Seemed safe enough. The passenger rolled down her window and asked where I was heading. I told her Crowsnest Pass, which is where the group would stop for the night. They said they were going as far as Frank, about 30 miles up the road. The driver got out and opened the tailgate for me to put my bike into the truck bed. When I squeezed into the cab of the truck with the two girls, I was enveloped in a cloud of stale cigarette smoke. Tiffany, the driver, had on a man's shirt with the sleeves cut off at the shoulders. She was wearing jeans and cowboy boots and looked as if she had broken a few bucking broncos in her day. Amber, the passenger, looked about the same, except she was wearing a tee shirt that was way too tight for her ample bosom. They both had that grizzled outdoors look of people that spend their day working horses and doing chores around the stable.

"How far ya goin' on that thing?" asked Amber, as she blew smoke my way.

"I hope I'm going to make it to Anchorage (cough, cough), if my knees don't blow up on me," I said.

"What's wrong with your knees?" asked Amber.

"I think I've got tendonitis. We rode over Going-to-the-Sun Highway in the rain a few days ago and…."

Tiffany said, "You rode over Going-to-the-Sun Highway? I bet you got some strong legs under them pant legs, eh?"

"Well…."

Amber reached over and gave my thigh a quick squeeze, "Oh, yeah! Like rocks!"

"About how much farther is it to Frank?" I asked, as I noticed Tiffany giving me the eye like a traveling salesman might do when he meets a pretty girl in a bar.

Amber said,"Oh, about another 10 or 15 miles. Hey, we're having a party tonight with some friends. Lotsa beer, eh? Wanna come?"

"Ah, well, I'm riding with nine others, and I'm, ah, supposed to, ah, cook dinner tonight (I had actually finished my cooking stint for another seven or eight days) and I, ah, need to meet them at Crowsnest Pass. They'll, ah, be counting on me to be there and have dinner cooked, ya know?"

Tiffany looked at me with what I thought was a gleam in her eyes. "I'm sure it would be worth your while. Are you suuure?"

She gave me the Western Canadian cowgirl version of a sultry look.

"I'm flattered. But I reallllly need to be there tonight to cook dinner."

We fell into an awkward quiet and rode the rest of the way in silence.

As I was getting my bike out of the back of the truck in Frank, Amber said, "Are you suuure you'd rather spend the evening with nine smelly guys eating dinner? Last chance."

"I'd better not." I mumbled.

"Suit yourself. Have a good ride, eh," said Tiffany. And they were gone.

The town of Frank didn't look to be much of a town and the road appeared to be cut through the middle of what looked like a huge boulder field that stretched from the mountains on one side of the road, to as far as the eye could see on the other side of the road. A little farther on there was a Province of Alberta sign that explained it all:

Frank Slide
April 29, 1903

"Disaster struck the town of Frank at 4:10 am April 29, 1903, when a gigantic wedge of limestone, 2,100 feet high, 3,000 feet wide and 500 feet thick, crashed down from Turtle Mountain.

Ninety million tons of rock swept over a mile of valley, destroying part of the town, taking 70 lives, and burying an entire mine plant and railway in approximately 100 seconds. The old town was located at the western edge of the slide where many cellars are still visible."

Frank was on the receiving end of another monumental tragedy in the 1920's when a mining disaster claimed over 150 lives.

I was standing smack in the middle of the avalanche field, and felt overwhelmingly vulnerable and mortal. The area was still and quiet. Standing amongst the rocks was like standing amongst thousands of tombstones. It was uncomfortable and I decided it was time to move on. I hopped on my bike and slowly finished the ride to Crowsnest Pass.

The group laughed at my hitchhiking experience over dinner, although John was incredulous that I didn't take Amber and Tiffany up on their party offer-or worse, that I didn't think to include him.

6

June 12–14

✦

535 miles from Missoula

The weather the next morning was in the 30's and rainy. We crossed into British Columbia and had a great eight-mile downhill from the pass. We spent the day sharing the road with large dump trucks going back and forth between various mines along the way. The roads were muddy from the truck tires and we were continually splashed with the grime from the roads. I managed to ride the whole seventy-two mile day without much knee discomfort, and we ended the day huddled in a grocery store in Jaffray, B.C., trying to warm up before our anticipated stay at the campground down the road.

I struck up a conversation with a guy in the store who had asked the usual questions of where we were going and where we had started. Turns out he was a P.E. teacher that liked to do a little bike riding of his own during the summer. He offered for us to stay the night at his house just a short ride down the road. His name was Glenn and he proved to be a very gracious and amiable host. His house was small, and the ten of us were scattered everywhere (floors, couches, hallways). We tried to be good house guests by cooking dinner and cleaning the house better than it was when we arrived.

It was hard to leave the next morning because it was 34F and we had a long day of riding ahead. We were to ride sixty-five miles to Canal Flats. Unbelievably, it started raining again as soon as we were back on the main road. We started calling it permadrizzle because there seemed to be no end to it. The air felt heavy.

Creaky knees again forced me to hitchhike. I stuck out my thumb and began pushing my bike in the cold rain. Amazingly, I was picked up by the first pick-up truck that passed. I was getting more accustomed to hitching a ride and was not nearly as anxious as I was during the first day of getting rides.

Hank, a welder by trade, was my ride for the next forty miles to Fort Steele. He was also an amateur inventor. I asked him what he had been working on.

"I've sent three inventions off for patent applications. The first is a flying car that uses large fans to move up or down, sideways, or backwards. It's gonna work fine, eh, but we lost the prototype in the Atlantic Ocean on its maiden flight. Sank right to the bottom. Pilot was lucky to get out, eh."

"Oops," I said.

"Yeah, no kidding! I spent three years on that machine. Now I'm trying to raise more money to build another."

"What's your second invention?"

"We're working on a new fuel type where one pound of coal combined with one pound of sugar, along with some other chemicals that I won't disclose, will burn for five and a half hours at a cost of 35 cents. I also believe we can configure the fuel to make a car to go 1,000 miles for about $7.00. Oil company won't like that, eh? They'll fight us tooth and nail."

"And number three?"

We've built an electric/magnetic engine that runs by the magnetic fields' centrifugal force."

Before I could get more explanation on the third invention, we were coming into the town of Fort Steele. The temperature was still in the low thirties and Hank said, "I hate to leave you here, but I think you'll find another ride to Canal Flats easy enough. Hardly anyone will leave someone walking by the side of the road in weather like this, eh?" And as I watched Hank pull away, it started to snow. Hard.

I rode/walked a couple of miles while the snow collected on top of my panniers. It was inconceivable to me that it could snow anywhere but Antarctica on June 13. There wasn't much traffic and I was contemplating my next move when a pink pick-up truck slowed to a stop and a guy leaned out of his window and said:

"Where ya heading?"

"Canal Flats!"

"I'm heading that way. Hop in."

Considering the weather, and the fact that within a few minutes I would resemble a snowman pushing a bike, I was very happy to have a ride, even if it was with a guy driving a pink pick-up truck. The truck appeared to be hand painted, in a shade of pink that should be reserved for French bordellos or little girl bedrooms. There were Pink Panther decals on both doors and a little Pink

Panther statue swinging from the rear-view mirror. The seats were upholstered in some sort of white fuzzy material, not unlike polar bear fur.

We drove through mining and logging country, and Seth, the truck's owner, didn't seem the least concerned about driving a hand painted pink pick-up truck. He was headed north to work in the oil fields because he was bored at home. Boredom wouldn't be an issue, I thought, when he drove the pink truck on site at the oil wells.

He let me out at a Texaco gas station/café at the intersection of the gravel road into Canal Flats and the main road north toward Radium Hot Springs. Canal Flats, a logging town, was to be our stop for the night. It was only about 11:00 AM and I expected the group to arrive at about 4:00 PM after the sixty-five mile ride from Jaffray. It was still snowing and the road had been slushy most of the last forty miles. The Texaco/café looked like a pretty good place to wait for the guys, and so I parked my bike, went inside, and found a quiet table near the counter. During the next several hours, I wrote post-cards, ate lunch, and continued my reading of *Zen and the Art of Motorcycle Maintenance.* I tried to be diligent in reading this book, but its larger (and smaller) meaning was pretty much lost on me, so I began reading my other book: *Night of the Grizzlies,* a book about bear attacks in Glacier National Park. We hadn't seen any bears there, but I assumed (hoped!) we'd see some as we got farther north.

In the afternoon, several people who had just traveled up the same road I had been on came into the café. One guy ambled over to me and asked, "Are you the guy riding with a large group of bikers from Montana?"

"That's me."

"Well, I saw your buddies at a store in Skookumchuck about thirty miles back. They got caught in the snow, eh, and decided to spend the night in a motel. They said if I saw you to let you know they'd see you tomorrow."

"Oh, well, ah, okay, thanks." I said, and the guy left.

This was not a good situation. I was thirty miles away from the group, had about fifteen dollars in my pocket, and no idea what to do next. At least it had stopped snowing.

It was Saturday afternoon, and Canal Flats was about to become the recreational hot spot for a bunch of rowdy loggers ready to booze it up after a long week in the woods.

Outside, at the gas pumps, the fun was already starting. A couple of guys in a white pick-up truck with monster tires had just filled their truck with gas and were now simultaneously riding their brakes and stomping the gas pedal. The big monster tires were spinning in place with a major squealing of tires and plumes of white smoke pouring off of them. They sat there for what seemed like minutes before the driver released the brake and the truck careened down the little road towards Canal Flats spewing gravel in all directions. The waitress in the café murmured at the spectacle of the monster truck and said, "It's going to be a wild time in town tonight, eh? It's payday, and those boys in the truck are going to blow all their money in one night."

I had an idea. I said to the waitress: "I'm kinda stuck in Canal Flats for the night since my riding partners got stuck in the snow. Do you know of a church in town that might be willing to let me spend the night in one of their Sunday school rooms?"

She said, "I don't know, it bein' Saturday night and all. They may not want someone to be sleeping in the sanctuary when the church-goers come in for Sunday school, eh?"

"Good point," I said, "do you have another suggestion? I don't have a lot of cash with me and couldn't afford anything too expensive"

"Well, there's the Columbia Bar in town. They have a hotel above the bar that is pretty cheap. It isn't very nice either."

As I pushed my bike down the gravel road towards Canal Flats, cars and pickups full of people were zooming by on the way into town for the festivities. Walking into Canal Flats was like walking into a western movie set. It had one fairly short main street with false front buildings on each side. There were wooden sidewalks raised up about six inches from the ground and what looked like rails for tying horses. It looked as if John Wayne or Robert Mitchum might ride into town looking for bad guys. Cars and trucks were parked everywhere.

The Columbia Hotel was at the far end of the street on the left, and as I came closer I noticed that there were swinging doors going into the bar. The outside of the hotel, painted a sort of faded blue, was old and weathered. The words "Columbia Bar and Hotel were painted in black on the window that faced the wooden sidewalk. Inside, there must have been a tremendous brawl taking place because I could hear yelling and what sounded like chairs and large amounts glass breaking.

The Columbia Hotel was logger's central and I wasn't going to stay there that Saturday night. No one had been in the street when I came into town, but now there was one obviously drunk young guy staggering my way down the sidewalk.

I said, "Excuse me, friend, do you know if there is a Mounted (Royal Canadian Mounted Police) Police headquarters here?"

He squinted at me and said, "What the f____ do we need the Mounties here for?"

"Ah, well, I was just looking for a place to spend the night, and I thought I could sleep at their headquarters."

He was getting belligerent and said, "Why don't you sleep in yer f____ing tent, faggot? That's why yer out here isn't it?"

He eyed me up and down and took several unbalanced steps towards me clenching and unclenching his fists.

He got within five feet, and without thinking, I reached down, pulled the almost two-foot long Zefal bike pump off my bike, and waved it in front of him like a billy club.

This unexpected action from me seemed to confuse the guy. He stopped, looked at the pump, shrugged, and turned to go into the Columbia Bar.

Now was the time to leave Canal Flats before he brought his buddies outside to finish the fight. I got on my bike and rode like my knees were in perfect shape. About halfway out of town the pick-up from the Texaco station came sliding back up the road. I got off my bike and headed for the ditch just as they shot past still slinging gravel. When the coast was clear, I headed for the main road with the intention of riding north until I found a good spot well off the road to camp. I passed the Texaco and within several hundred yards came upon a British Columbia Forest Ranger Station, where two guys stood outside talking. I mustered my courage and asked them if they knew of a good place to spend the night. One of them said, "Sure. We have a dormitory. Stay here, and you can even sleep in a bed!" Canal Flats wasn't so bad after all.

At mid-morning the next day, my biking buddies appeared just as I was polishing off brunch at the café. We traded stories. They were amazed at my near bar-fight story, and I was envious of their motel stay with hot showers. They kept riding towards Radium Hot Springs, Sinclair Pass, and then to our stopping point, MacLeod Meadows. I stuck out my thumb and grudgingly pushed my bike.

A retired Canadian Olympic skier named John picked me up before too long and offered to take me to the top of Sinclair Pass. This was a great deal since it was about five miles to the top of the pass and I could almost coast down the other side to MacLeod Meadows. We talked about my knee problems and John told me he had had several bad knee injuries during his skiing career. The best thing for my knees, he said, would be to soak them in pools of really hot water for a while then immediately soak them in pools of really cold water, and to keep doing this for about an hour. He said that he was a part owner of a private club in Fairmont Hot Springs and that I could be his guest to soak in their hot and cold pools.

As he left me at the locker room, he said, "I'll see you in an hour. Oh, and you might want to take a good long shower…with soap. You need it."

The top of Sinclair Pass with the Canadian Rockies as a backdrop.

For the next hour I sat in one pool for a few minutes, then switched to the other. This, apparently, was the miracle cure. It was amazing how much alternating between hot and cold pools helped my knees and also how it improved my attitude. The day was (finally!) sunny and warm, and the pools were just all-around fabulous. After my time in the pools and a good soapy shower we loaded up and headed for the top of Sinclair Pass. The road turned toward the northeast, and we passed Radium Hot Springs, a hot springs made into a public pool. The road up to the top of the pass was gorgeous. When we got to the top it was sunny, and the view across the valley of the Canadian Rockies was magnificent. I bid John a sad goodbye and gave him my heartfelt thanks for his kindness and hospitality. I figured I would wait for the guys at the top of the pass and ride with them down the other side to MacLeod Meadows.

Typically, it wasn't long before a cloud formed over the pass and it started raining. I didn't think the guys would try and ride up the pass in the rain and would probably find a place to camp in Radium Hot Springs, so I hitched a ride back down with a girl in a pick-up. She obviously wanted to be hospitable but was looking at me like I was an axe murderer and appeared very uncomfortable. When we were 4/5 of the way down the five mile road over the pass we passed John and Arnold on their way up. I got out and figured I'd hitch back up again. Only this time no one picked me up. I had been to the top, came back down most of the way, now I had to walk back up. Four miles. Everyone in my group passed me as I was walking and they all had a good laugh at my extra walk. They waited for me at the top and we rode together to MacLeod Meadows, a total of fifty-six miles for the day.

7

June 14–17

◆

665 miles from Missoula

Next morning we headed to Lake Louise, sixty-five miles away, for our first rest day since Waterton. We had stayed in a campground that was right in the middle of bear country. We knew this because there were signs everywhere that warned against leaving food out or in tents, lest the bears would think it their good fortune to happen onto a buffet provided by unsuspecting campers. The campground wasn't yet open for the season (we expected it would be), but we pushed our bikes around the gate and began setting up camp. We figured on safety in numbers, and all camped inside the open air shelter, sleeping on top of picnic tables. Picnic tables are not meant for restful sleep. All of us were a little wary as we closed our eyes and probably slept a little lighter than normal in case a bear tried to warm itself inside one of our sleeping bags.

The group got an early start, and I began thumbing and pushing down the road. A ride picked me up after I had walked about five miles and offered to take me to Lake Louise. The driver, Jay, was a Forest Service employee on his way to a job near Lake Louise. He was driving a dented, mud-spattered, green Forest Service pick-up truck with large wheels, so it was much higher than a normal pick-up. While we made small talk, I noticed the terrain changing from hilly to flat and marshy. Perfect place to see a bear, I thought.

"Look there!" He yelled.

Startled, I said, "What? Where!?"

"Over there! A baby moose!"

It was true. A baby moose was galumping towards us with what looked like playful curiosity. Jay slowed to a stop and the moose loped right up to my window, which was partially open, and stuck his snout in breathing loudly. The first thing that surprised me was how tall baby moose are. He was able to look right in the window even though we were very high off the ground. The second thing is that baby moose have very bad breath and tend to slobber. A lot.

The moose snuffled around the truck for a few minutes as we watched, pausing to smear moose snot on Jay's window, and then, apparently satisfied, headed off in the direction from which he had come. Jay told me that the baby moose was probably about 800 pounds now, and would grow to 1,700-1,800 pounds by maturity. I was amazed to see something so large not in a zoo.

Jay dropped me off at a hotel in the townsite of Lake Louise, just down the mountain from the world-famous Chateau Lake Louise. After several hours of waiting, which included two milkshakes, a piece of plum pie, and a piece of apple pie, the group showed up. We went to the local campground that would be our home for the next couple of days. The weather had been nice all day, and John, Steve, Dale, and Tim had ridden without their shirts. Now, in the evening, it was rainy and the temperature had dropped about twenty-five degrees. We had a quick dinner in the rain and then a made hasty retreat to our tents for the night. At my height of 6 ' 4 ", it was awkward, at best, to have to climb into a tent and sleeping bag in good weather. It became more complicated in bad weather. Soon, I perfected the speed entry into my tent in order keep the rain and mosquitoes out. Once inside, it became an Olympic gymnastics event to skooch around getting wet clothes and shoes off before they got the sleeping bag wet. Invariably, the inside of the tent was freezing and was oh, so, uncomfortable in the brief transition between getting clothes off and sliding into the sleeping bag.

I was always amazed at how rapidly the sleeping bag warmed from my body heat. It was very toasty on even the coldest nights. The inside of the tent always became about fifteen degrees warmer, too. The very hardest part, though, was getting out of a warm sleeping bag on a cold, wet morning. It was, essentially, everything in reverse. Only faster and more shocking to the system.

For our day of rest at Lake Louise, our plan was to get up, eat, do a weeks worth of laundry, take showers, and visit the Chateau Lake Louise up the mountain from our campsite. In 1882, Tom Wilson, an employee of the Canadian Pacific Railroad, was camping at Laggan Station (Lake Louise Station, now) when he heard what he thought was thunder. His Stoney Indian guides told him the "thunder" came from a big white mountain high above the "lake of little fishes." The next morning he became the first non-native to see what is now called Lake Louise. "For some time we sat and smoked and gazed at the gem of beauty beneath the glacier." Wilson called the "gem" Emerald Lake. In 1884, it was renamed Lake Louise in honor of Princess Louise Caroline Alberta, daughter of Queen Victoria and wife of Canada's governor general.

The Chateau began as "a hotel for the adventurer and alpinist," according to the vision of the general manager of Canadian Pacific Railroad, Cornelius van Horne. Built on the shores of Lake Louise, in 1890, two years after its sister hotel, The Banff Springs Hotel, it was a simpler chalet catering to no more than one hundred guests during a summer season. In the early 1900's over 5,000 guests visited the chalet, causing enough demand to expand the chalet, from a capacity of a dozen guests to 240. In 1924, a fire destroyed much of the old building. Within a year a new eight-story brick hotel was built by Canadian Pacific Railway, and the hotel was renamed Chateau Lake Louise.

Pete, Dale, and I left our campsite with the idea if hitching up the mountain to the Chateau and spending time looking around the grounds and hotel. The road up to the chateau from town was about three miles and very heavily traveled, so we didn't anticipate any difficulty getting a ride.

Well, it wasn't difficult for some people to get rides....

We had started walking upward with our thumbs out. Soon, a car pulled over and the driver said he had room for only two more. We decided to do "Rock, Paper, Scissor" to see who the odd man out would be.

That would be me.

Pete and Dale smirked and got in the car. I continued walking and thumbing. No other cars even slowed down.

Eventually, I came into sight of what had to be the most magnificent location for a hotel in the world. The Chateau was a sprawling eight-story French style hotel nestled between mountains that were amongst the most beautiful the Canadian Rockies had to offer. The lake was an amazing color of turquoise, that I had never seen anywhere else but Bermuda. It was a color like the turquoise one sees on jewelry from the desert southwest of America, but much more attractive. At the far end of the 1.5-mile long lake hung Victoria Glacier, still full of snow in early June. Mountains on the left side of the lake rose so precipitously out of the water so that a slippery footed mountain climber might tumble from great heights into the cold, glacier-fed water. Red canoes dotted the lake as tourists paddled with more enthusiasm than skill. To the right, a much used trail skirted the lake and led to the area around Victoria Glacier. There was a large grassy area between the Chateau and the lake where dozens of people sat and admired the view.

Pete and I hiked part way down the trail for a first-rate view of the lake with the Chateau behind it. We turned and walked back through the gracious hotel admiring the shops, savoring the sumptuous smells from the restaurants, and suddenly feeling very dirty and underdressed. We beat a hasty retreat and headed back down the mountain to our own kind-smelly and over-bearded. This time, I was able to catch a ride.

After a couple of nice relaxing days in Lake Louise, it was time to continue northward. We had clean clothes, rested muscles, and renewed enthusiasm. I had all of those, of course, plus the added benefit of being able to tell that the hitch-hiking, rest days, and hot and cold pools in Fairmont Hot Springs had done my knees some good. I also started the morning and afternoon regimen of taking a couple of aspirin to help reduce swelling and pain.

We headed out to the Icefields Parkway, and I intended to ride as far as I could. The Parkway, sometimes has been called one of the world's most spectacular highway s, is the approximat ely 150-mile ribbon of road that connects Banff

The group on the second of several crossings of the continental divide.

National Park to the south and Jasper National Park to the north. Both parks are huge. Banff National Park is 2,564 square miles, which is larger than Delaware, while Jasper National Park, at 10,878 square miles, is larger than Maryland. For much of the way, the road parallels the continental divide and passes scenery that is unimagin-able in its beauty and sweeping grandeur. Our ride for the next several days would takes us from subalpine forest to alpine meadows, to montane forest, and back again. We would cross the highest point of the parkway, Bow Summit, at 6,780 feet. We would follow the Mistaya, Sunwapta, and Athabasca Rivers and cross the famous Saskatchewan River at Saskatchewan Crossing. We would pass Bow and Peyto Lakes, both famous for their otherworldly turquoise waters sur-rounded by jagged mountain peaks. We would pass Crowfoot Glacier and the Columbia Icefields, where the largest glaciers in the Canadian Rockies are located. Lastly, we would be pedaling through prime animal country in which we might see black bears and grizzly bears, moose, elk, mountain caribou, mountain goats, and bighorn sheep.

I started off slowly, and the others were quickly out of sight. The weather was cold, cloudy, and threatening snow. While my knees were actually feeling good, I was concerned that I might undo the healing that had taken place during the last few days, so I continued to ride gingerly and made it about twenty-five miles by the time the clouds dropped and it started to snow. During the ride, I noticed that the mountains had heavy snow near their tops and that it was possible to see the various layers of rock just below where the snow started all the way down to the tree line. Since it was now snowing and hailing hard, I figured it was as good a time as any to start hitching. Shortly, a nice guy from Fernie (not far from Crowsnest Pass), named Al, picked me up and offered to take me all the way to Jasper. I got out at after fifty-five miles at the Rampart Creek Youth Hostel, our home for the night, thanked Al, and quickly pushed the bike up the hill to the hostel to wait for the others. Al and I had just seen a large black bear near the road shortly before we got to the hostel; as the bear lumbered off into the woods, he gave us a view of his bare bear backside.

The hostel consisted of a couple of small buildings that held only six bunk beds each. There was also a small cabin for the caretaker of the hostel. The windows of all three buildings were covered with heavy screen intended to keep bears out. I noticed that a couple of screens had been forcibly pulled away from the brackets holding them to the walls and that there were big gouges visible on the wall from bear claws. There was a cleared area in front of the buildings with a small fire pit. Across the clearing there was a stream roiling out of a narrow canyon, which is where we were to get our water. A porta-john to be used by anyone and everyone stood at the edge of the clearing. Ian, the caretaker, lived there for free during the summer but had no running water, electricity, or food, which he had to provide himself. He also had to contend with intruding bears. When I remarked that he seemed to be getting the short end of the deal, he said he wouldn't have it any other way.

When the others arrived, we played Frisbee in the clearing and gawked at the magnificent scenery. The weather had almost cleared, and the sun was beautifully reflecting on the cliff next to the hostel and highlighting the snow-capped range across the road. There was an interesting formation called Cleopatra's Needle on top of a distant peak that was shaped, well, like a needle. It was probably 200 feet tall, part of it was bathed in sunlight and part of it covered in snow squalls.

Both Pete and Tom decided to quit the trip in Jasper, which was now only two riding days away. I had noticed for several days that they had been distancing themselves from the group and had become unusually (for them) quiet. The group, in turn, had begun distancing itself from them. It was as if the groups arm had become diseased and the group was intent on cutting the arm off before the disease spread to others. It was becoming awkward at meals because they were ready to move on, and the group, without really meaning to, had subconsciously started looking on, too.

In truth, the constant knee pain of so many days almost made me fleetingly consider quitting the trip as well. I didn't want to leave the trip because I knew that I needed to follow through with the commitment to ride to Alaska; otherwise, I would regret it as I got older. "Yep, grandson, I was on an epic bike ride to Alaska, but I finished only 1/6th of the ride." I didn't want that.

But I found myself in an awkward position, too. I had had to hitchhike so many days that while I was *part* of the group, I was not really *in* the group. The group was sympathetic about my knee problems and the necessity to hitchhike but I also hadn't really "proved" myself in their eyes. I *had* to finish the trip for myself and also because I didn't want to become a "*persona non grata*" like Pete and Tom had become during their last days on the trip.

8

June 17–20

✦

747 miles from Missoula

Amazingly, I woke up the next morning with no tenderness or pain whatsoever in my knees and, needless to say, this was an agreeable development both physically and mentally. Nevertheless, I decided not to push my good luck just yet, and I started thumbing as soon as we left Rampart Creek. Almost immediately, I was picked up by a man driving a road-worn looking van. When he opened the side door of the van to let me in, I was surprised to see three women sitting in a circle on the floor of the van. There were no other seats besides the driver seat and passenger seat. The driver was a professor from the University of Wisconsin on vacation with his wife and his mother, who appeared ancient. They were all from New Delhi, India, originally, and the women were wearing very pretty saris of vibrant colors that looked impossibly out of place in the wilds of Canada. Mary, the other lady, was the professor's research assistant. She appeared to be about my age, and she looked as if she had stepped off the front page of an L.L. Bean catalogue. She had red hair, was dressed impeccably for hiking, and had the added benefit of being very attractive (a very big plus for someone riding with nine other guys!).

The inside of the van was covered with the detritus of long-distance travel: suitcases stacked to the ceiling in back, a makeshift clothesline with hanging clothes, shoes, sandals, and hiking boots stuffed into little nooks. I climbed in to join the three ladies sitting cross-legged on the van floor. They had been traveling jammed up like this for ten days and didn't appear any the worse because of it. When they asked me the usual questions about my trip, the conversation was translated to the mother who appeared to speak no English. Every time she heard the translation, she would look at me, raise her eyebrows, give an appreciative nod, and say, "oohh." They were extremely nice people, and we enjoyed a sort of warm bonhomie as we left Banff National Park and crossed into Jasper National Park.

When we reached the Columbia Icefields, we got out for an early lunch at the small Icefields Chalet overlooking the toe of the Athabasca Glacier. We had suddenly arrived in one of the most unusual and geologically active regions in the northern hemisphere. The Columbia Icefield is the largest glacial area in the Northern Hemisphere south of the Arctic Circle. It straddles the borders of Alberta and British Columbia at the continental divide, while it joins Banff National Park to Jasper National Park. The icefield (233 sq. miles) is almost four times as large as the city of Washington, D.C. (61 sq. miles), and spawns six outlet valley glaciers: Athabasca, Saskatchewan, Dome, Columbia, Castleguard, and Stutfield.

On the Athabasca Glacier, the glacial ice is a little over 1,000 feet thick, and since glaciers are always moving, it takes 300 years for the ice to move from the glacial headwall to the toe, 2,600 feet away; an astoundingly slow 2.5 inches a year!

Mt. Snow Dome, next to the Athabasca Glacier, is known as a hydrological apex because it is only one of two locations in the world where meltwater from its summit flows to three oceans, the other hydrological apex being in Siberia. Meltwater from the top of the dome flows into the Atlantic via the North Saskatchewan River, to the Pacific via the Columbia River, and to the Arctic Ocean via the Athabasca and Mackenzie Rivers.

Meanwhile, Mary and I were getting along famously. She had invited me (with a nod from the professor) to join them on the rest of their vacation. Again, I was tempted to leave the trip, and this time it was because of Mary's green eyes and not because of my knees. Every time Mary looked at me, it made me want to join their vacation in the worst way. This was getting ridiculous, dadgummit! I couldn't do it. There was no way. It wouldn't happen.

I told her I'd think about it.

So, as a way of prolonging our time together, Mary and I decided we'd like to take a tour of the Athabasca Glacier by sno-cat, which is kind of like a bus perched on top of bulldozer tracks. The tours started from a small building at the top of a steep and narrow road cut through the rocks dug up by the right edge of the Athabasca Glacier. And off the five of us went in the road-worn van. Because the road was built on unstable soil, it was bumpy and rolly, and as it got within ½ mile of the sno-cat chalet, the road slanted steeply upward. The last 100 feet were so steep that our van couldn't pull the hill, even in its lowest gears. We were precariously stuck in the middle of the road only 100 feet from the top. Backing down would have been foolhardy; the road was too steep and narrow. Going up was going to take some help. We all climbed out of the van to make it lighter and the professor gunned the motor. The van shuddered and went nowhere. He gingerly backed down a little and then tried again. Still the van didn't move. Panic started to show on his face because he was seemingly out of any options other than trying to back down the hill.

Out of nowhere, a bulldozer chugged up to the front of the van. A guy got off and said he would be happy to put a chain on the van and pull it the rest of the way up the hill. For twenty dollars! He had us over a barrel, we couldn't go up, and it was too risky to back down. The professor, Mary, and I split the cost, and he pulled the van the last 100 feet to the top. I sidled over to the guy and whispered:

"How many times a day do you have to do this?"

He said, "Maybe twenty on a good day. Not a bad way to make a little extra cash, eh?"

Mary and I bought tickets and climbed aboard the sno-cat. The tour took us directly down onto the ice along a carefully delineated trail to an area that looked like it had been graded by a bulldozer. This "parking/viewing" area was bounded on the edges by orange cones. The driver/guide admonished us to stay within the area of the cones because the area outside might not be safe. She said, "The glacier is always active and there might be crevasses or holes you could fall into. People sometimes hike the glacier without guides, tumble into a hole or crevasse, and get really hurt or freeze to death before they can be rescued. Occasionally, someone will just disappear and is never seen again. We've found holes and crevasses that are over three hundred feet deep."

This was an attention getter for us and the other tourists in the cleared space.

The air was cold. We were bundled up and we could see our breath. The sun was so bright that the reflection on the ice was almost blinding. We stepped around puddles of ice-cold water. Rivulets of water ran downhill around us from the glacier headwall. Think about this: We were standing on ice one thousand feet thick. If the Empire State Building was buried beneath us, we would probably be able to only see the tip of its radio tower sticking up through the ice. Snow that fell on the top of the ice would take seven hundred years to sink to the rock bottom under our feet. The temperature in the winter has been recorded as low as-80F and the icefields can receive as much as twenty feet of snow yearly.

Painfully, as much as I wanted to go with Mary and her friends, I knew I had to finish the ride, and I hated to tell her that on the short trip back to the sno-cat chalet. I had a pit in my stomach. She looked disappointed. It might have been my imagination. We rode the rest of the way in companionable silence.

My knees were fine, and I decided I'd ride the rest of the way to our stop for the night at Honeymoon Lake. Mary and I hugged and traded addresses with promises to get in touch after the summer. I shook hands with the professor and sadly waved goodbye to his family. His mother smiled, gently touched my arm, and said something to me in her native language. The professor also smiled and translated that she had just given me her wish for my safe journey. They were going to stay there for a few more minutes so I saddled up and pointed my bike down the steep, curvy, rolly road.

The next couple of miles rated as the scariest, most out-of-control downhill ride of the whole trip.

Flat tires were a constant annoyance.
Here, Tim fixes one while we lend moral support.

I started slow at the top of the steepest part but quickly found that the road was too steep to ride slow; I would topple over the front at this speed. My loaded bike weighed about 80 pounds, I weighed about 185 pounds, and my bike was not the most maneuverable one around. I just pointed it downhill and hoped I could hang on without going over the front or crashing into the boulders lining the road. Downward I flew, the wind whipping through my hair (I had stupidly left my helmet in my front pannier), and the boulders flashing past. Just then, I hit the rolly part of the road at about forty miles an hour and was almost pitched off. My right foot came out of my toe clips and I was barely staying in control. There were some good-sized rocks that had fallen on the road and I was on them too soon to swerve. I couldn't have done much anyway because the road was too narrow for much evasive action. I clipped the edge and my wheel skidded slightly but I was able to catch it before I went down. I blew by a car chugging slowly up towards the chalet. My mouth was open in a silent, "Aaaahhhh," and my jaws were flapping in the wind. And then, suddenly, it was over. The road flattened out and I coasted to an easy stop at the intersection with the Icefields Parkway, breathing heavily and shaking with a mixture of adrenaline and fear.

The thirty-five or so miles to Honeymoon Lake were mostly downhill to flat coming out of the icefields, and I rode slowly with no knee problems. The campground at Honeymoon Lake was not officially open until the next day, so I went around the gate as we did at MacLeod Meadows.

The campground was situated next to the most beautiful and tranquil lake I had ever seen. Across the lake, dark green forests seemed to melt into the surface of the clear water. Jagged mountains erupted from the forest and were capped with snow. The sky crackled a sharp blue. It was cathedral quiet. There was no wind. I wandered around the shoreline to a dock I had seen and sat on the end looking across the lake. I was conflicted and I needed to work out in my mind what I intended to do. I had been a bit shaken by my willingness to leave the trip and head off on vacation with perfect strangers. I was saddened that Pete and Tom actually *were* going to leave the trip the next day, and I had been almost ready to hang it up because of knee problems. I needed time to reflect on the trip and to decide whether I was serious enough about it to finish it.

I sat for a long time, my mind a jumble of feelings and emotions. Stay? Go? Try and catch up with Mary? Gradually, a resolute feeling came over me and I knew I would finish the trip. Plus, I had decided that I really wanted to see Mt. McKinley in Alaska. This would be my visual reward.

The group trickled in after their sixty mile ride, and we started the normal evening process of cooking, eating, discussing the days ride, and what to expect on the next day's ride. I announced that I intended to ride the last few miles to Jasper tomorrow and that after the planned rest day there, I thought I would be able to riding full-time again.

It was an easy thirty-two mile ride to Jasper. The road mostly followed the Athabasca River and cut through some lush forests. I took it slow and got off the bike at several spots along the way-once at Athabasca Falls to take some pictures, and once to follow an elk into the woods to try to get a close-up photo. In retrospect, this wasn't a very bright thing to do. The elk probably weighed 600 pounds, had a full head of antlers, and could have really done me some damage if he had been so inclined. It seemed like a good idea at the time.

Jasper, Alberta, was at the northern end of our trip up the Icefields Parkway. There we would turn northwestward on Route 16, the Yellowhead Highway. But first, we were going to enjoy a rest-day and set up camp in the Whistler Campground, just south of Jasper. Tim had ridden with me from Honeymoon Lake and we had decided the first important task was to go to the A&W Drive-In in town and get a milkshake...or three. We then found a coin-operated laundry with showers. After four days, it was good to wash clothes and have a shower.

That night we went to a nature talk about the local population of bears. The show was humorous, the park ranger gave a slide show about bears stuck in trash cans and standing on top of tourist cars with the people inside. He also made it clear that bears were dangerous and were becoming more familiar with people, and, therefore, less afraid to come looking for easy food. He showed a funny slide of an alarmingly knuckleheaded woman who tried to get a really close-up picture of a bear, and then punched it in the nose when it wouldn't stand still for the photo. The bear, apparently surprised, walked into the forest to the great good fortune of the knuckleheaded lady.

Whistler Campground is the first place where we were required to hang our food, supposedly out of reach of bears. The ranger said that an enterprising (and really hungry) bear would still be able to get into suspended food but that it was still the best deterrent.

The next morning, Steve, Arnold, and I rode the tramway to the top of Mt. Whistler for the birds-eye view of the Jasper Valley from about 9,000 feet. At our vantage-point, we could see the Icefields Parkway heading south, the road to Edmonton heading east, and the Yellowhead Highway heading northwest. The valley was "T" shaped and framed by snowcapped mountains. Jasper was in the middle of the "T". It was a glorious view. The rest of the day was spent sleeping, eating, doing bike maintenance, and catching up on letter writing.

Because Pete and Tom were leaving the next day, we were trying to be chipper, and chatty, but it actually fell flat and came across in a forced way. It was like being at a funeral home where everyone is trying to sound cheerful for the family of the deceased. We hated to see them go, but the group had already had time to become accustomed to their departure.

At breakfast the next day we all said our goodbyes. Tom was going to ride his bike to Calgary and then fly back to New Mexico. He would be riding solo back down the Icefields Parkway, then eastward to Calgary, a distance somewhat more than 200 miles. Pete would be riding a train eastward from Jasper, get off north of Wisconsin, and ride back to Green Bay, a bike ride he guessed to be about 250 miles. We rode together down the campground access road and then split in our various directions. I watched them ride off into the distance, and then I turned onto the Yellowhead Highway, left Alberta, and crossed back into British Columbia for the next segment of our ride.

9

June 21–23

✦

944 miles from Missoula

Today, for the first time since Going-to-the-Sun Highway, I rode the whole distance! Our ride was about fifty-five miles, mostly flat, with a few hills to keep us interested, though the first thirty minutes of the ride was into a pretty stiff headwind. Henry and I rode together at a slow pace that matched his normal pace and my physical therapy pace. We talked about the departure of Pete and Tom, and Henry became philosophical, saying "It's all part of the experience."

Most everything was "all part of the experience" with Henry. He was 63 years old and had seen it all. I had noticed that he was remarkable at pacing himself, always making it into camp right before dinner (unless he was one of the cooks, then he picked up the pace and made it early). He frequently talked about "stopping to smell the roses," and spending time with people he met along the way. He had become our unofficial trip ambassador and never failed to draw an appreciative crowd whenever he stopped. There were many times when I heard him expounding on the physical and mental benefits of bike riding to overweight adults and teens, many with cigarettes dangling precariously from their mouths. He was not above chastising them for smoking, either. He knew from experience; he had been overweight and smoked, too, in years past.

Little kids, especially, were drawn to him like some bike-riding Captain Kangaroo. He would prop his bike against a wall or a tree, sit down cross legged, and tell stories to them about his riding experiences. Little old ladies tended to follow him around and were enthralled by his attention. In a time when most people didn't wear bike helmets, he always wore his. He was invariably polite and friendly, although he could be snappish if provoked or if he thought someone was talking B.S. He could also be a little spacey, sometimes drifting off into a far-off land while you were talking to him. He had the advantage over all of us in that he had a world of life experience. All in all, he was a very agreeable riding partner.

Once, during our ride to Mt. Robson, we happened upon two elk wandering across the road. Henry, daydreaming about something, almost ran into one of them. The elk looked at Henry with a "for gosh sakes, watch where you're going" look. Luckily, they had not the least bit of interest in us and continued into the woods next to the road.

My knees worked like they were supposed to, and became tired only near the end of the ride. We crossed the boundary of Alberta and British Columbia at Yellowhead Pass, an important early fur trading route, and entered Mt.Robson Provincial Park.

The crowning jewel of the park is Mt. Robson, towering a breathtaking 12, 972 feet into the air, and holding the distinction of being the tallest mountain in the Canadian Rockies. It looks immense from the south side because it has an almost sheer face of over 9,000 feet; and the view from the road makes it appear as if it is separate from other nearby peaks. The north side of the mountain conceals an enormous glacier system that may be reached only by hiking. The mighty Berg Glacier is located in this glacier system and is notable for being one of the few advancing glaciers in the Canadian Rockies.

W.B. Cheadle, a British explorer, described the mountain in 1863: "On every side the mighty heads of snowy hills crowded round, whilst, immediately behind us, a giant among giants, and immeasurably supreme, rose Robson's peak…We saw its upper portion dimmed by a necklace of light, feathery clouds, beyond which its painted apex of ice, glittering in the morning sun, shot up into the blue heaven above." Oddly, the source of the mountain's name has never been confirmed. It could be a shortening of Robertson, a Hudson's Bay trapper who had been trapped in the region himself. Local Indians called the mountain *Yuh-hai-has-hun*, the "Mountain of the Spiral Road," alluding to very visible rock, resembling a road, that seems to climb its way to the summit. Because it is such a difficult mountain to climb, it wasn't scaled until 1913; it is still a serious challenge to climbers.

At dinner, as we were eating the first meal since Pete and Tom left, I realized that the tension of the past couple of weeks was gone. The group had had a big weight of uncertainty lifted from its collective neck and the mood was noticeably brighter. Still, it was a shame they left.

The Yellowhead Highway is a tribute to the nickname of the early 18th-century blond explorer, Peter Hastination, or maybe it was Francois Decoigne. No one is sure. A route crossing four Canadian Provinces, it begins its route from

Portage La Prairie, in Manitoba, all the way to Prince Rupert and the Queen Charlotte Islands on the British Columbia coast.

From Tete Jaune Cache (near Mt. Robson, and also named for one of the aforementioned explorers) the road slices through the Cariboo Mountains to the small logging city of Prince George. From there the road continues westward through the Fraser Plateau, the Bulkely River Valley, and the Skeena River Valley, on the way to the coastal town of Prince Rupert. The town of Vanderhoof, about sixty miles west of Prince George, is considered the geographical center of British Columbia, and is named for a Chicago publicist hired to promote the area in the early twentieth century.

We would be heading west on this road for the next nine days, then we would make our big turn north onto the gravel Stewart-Cassiar Highway at Kitwanga.

Drizzle at breakfast turned into sunshine for the ride to Goat River, seventy-six miles away. We had an immediate one mile uphill (tough going after breakfast!) from Tete Jaune Cache and lucked into a tailwind all the way to McBride, a distance of fifty miles. Steve and I were cooking for the night, so we made a side trip to a little grocery store in McBride, where we bought ingredients to make grilled cheese sandwiches and fruit salad. We had to carry the food the last twenty-six miles to our stopping point, Goat River. There was a really steep downhill into Goat River and, across the bridge, I could see the equally steep uphill out of Goat River. Now here a thought occurred to me that had somehow escaped me my whole life prior to this day: Roads that cross rivers almost always have a great downhill into the river valley but one has to pay the piper on the climb out. By the same token, roads that parallel rivers are usually nice, easy, and without major hills. You may say, "Well, duh," but this is something that is not at all obvious while riding in a car, but is that *very* obvious while riding an eighty-pound bike.

We met another biker, a girl, 22ish, riding from Vancouver eastward (she wasn't sure where yet, just riding east). Her name was Becky, and she was from California. We all thought she was beautiful and very naïve to be riding by herself. We wished her well as she headed out of the Goat River Valley.

Most places we stayed were campgrounds with at least a few facilities. Occasionally, we just pulled off and threw our tents up in rest areas or beside the road in what is best described as primitive camping. That night's campsite had no bathrooms, shelter, or running water. Just as we finished dinner, a cold permadrizzle set in. It had been a gloriously warm day and it was the first time since Seely Lake that I had had my parka off. Sadly, we headed for an early bedtime even though there was plenty of daylight left.

The steep uphill from Goat River was our wake-up call the next day and set the tone for what was mostly a day of hills. The weather was changeable, sun and rain, most of the day. Henry and I rode together again and had another great day of animal watching. At least I did; Henry barely avioded a really close encounter, again.

We were riding along and a mother moose and baby crossed the road a hundred feet in front of us. They were magnificent. The mother was huge and the baby was maybe six feet tall and all legs. Mindful of the warning we had received about mother moose, we stopped and let them pass. It was almost overwhelming to see something so majestic in such close proximity.

Later in the ride, we rounded a bend and unexpectedly came upon two black bears on the side of the road. They were in a seated position, facing each other, like at a fancy tea party, with their legs dangling off the road's shoulder. Henry never saw them, even though he rode within fifteen feet of them. I slammed on my brakes and came off my seat so fast that I came close to straddling the handlebar stem. I yelled at Henry, who didn't hear me, and tried to get my camera out for a picture. By the time I was able to get the camera out of my handlebar bag, the bears had skedaddled into the woods, and Henry was a good ways up the road, blissfully unaware of how close he had come to about 700 pounds of black bear.

Hungry, we stopped at a little restaurant in the middle of nowhere (it was the only thing we saw in the 100-miles between McBride and Prince George) and had milkshakes and mixed berry pie.

When we got to the Purden Lake campground after sisty-six miles, the weather was warm again and all of us went skinny dipping to celebrate crossing the 1,000-mile mark of the trip. There wasn't a very private location for dipping, so we had to post a lookout and intended to get in and out very quickly. It was a rather comical sight after the lookout gave the okay, for each of us to disrobe and run across the rocky shore into near frigid water. We had planned to take a *quick* swim. Unfortunately, a family of four walked up to take pictures of the lake. They stayed, and staayed and staaaaayed, and wanted to know all about our bike trip. We were full of cheerful chattering. Obviously, none of us would dare to come out of chest deep water and I thought we were all going to die of hypothermia before they left. When we were finally able to make our escape, we sprinted back to our clothes and hurried to get dressed before someone else showed up and we ended up in somebody's slide show. After dinner, I noticed that the sky was totally blue for the first time since we left Missoula, almost 1,000 miles back.

10

June 24–25

✦

1,042 miles from Missoula

The weather gods were smiling on us on our thirty-six mile ride the next day to Prince George. Nothing but sunshine! The road out of the campground was the roughest ride of the day, but we had some hills and a headwind that made the ride tougher than it should have been. The day's ride will always be highlighted, however, by the logging trucks and the insanely dangerous dash across the bridge going into Prince George.

Here's what happened.

The road between McBride and Prince George was heavily traveled by large logging trucks and they frequently passed us on the narrow, two-lane Yellowhead Highway. We were used to being passed, of course, by all kinds of vehicles: cars, tractor-trailers, motorcycles, and buses. Most of those vehicles gave us a wide berth in the road. This wasn't always the case with the logging trucks, however, and in my opinion, these trucks were the scariest of all. The drivers were good, but they drove fast and passed closer than any others.

When something small like a car passes, there is a whistling sound and some wind from the car blows you a bit. This is usually only a nuisance, unless the car passes too close for comfort. Canadian car drivers were invariably courteous, so this was a rare occurrence. But when a logging truck passed, one had to really be on his toes. Usually, if lucky, I could hear the truck coming up behind me and could ease over toward the wide emergency strip that's part of all Canadian roads and let them pass by. Sometimes, a truck was upon me before I knew there was one there. This was scary because a speeding truck produces a lot of buffeting wind, and this really affected our bikes. I would hear this big whooshing sound and then the truck would blow by. Then I could feel a sucking sensation pulling the bike towards the rear tires. This was unnerving until I got used to it and could compensate by leaning away from the wind pull. Sometimes there was another truck following closely behind the first and this was the scariest and most dangerous of all. The first truck would pass and I had to be careful not to be sucked by the wind of the passing truck back out into the road only to be blasted by the next truck. One learned about these things only by experience and by nearly getting flattened by following trucks.

Garry told us to wait at the bridge before crossing the wide Fraser River into Prince George. The bridge, he said, was about a mile long, very narrow, and heavily traveled by logging trucks. It was a short ride from Purden Lake, and we all arrived within minutes of each other at the bridge. We pulled off the road and Garry gave us his plan to get safely across.

"This is what you need to do. We rode this bridge last year and it was the most frightening part of the trip. The bridge is narrow and has grating most of the way across, meaning you can see the river below and is hard to ride on with bike tires. Trucks tried to pass us while we were on the bridge last year and a couple of the bikers nearly wrecked.

"I think the best way to cross it is to wait until there is a big break in traffic and then each person ride individually across. Ride like crazy, and try to stay in the middle of the road so no one will be able pass you on the bridge. Wait for everyone to get across, and we'll ride to our campsite together. Good luck"

It felt as if we were The Light Brigade charging into calamity.

We waited as we watched trucks race past us onto the bridge. You could hear the mournful whine of their tires as they rolled across the grating.

Suddenly, there was a break in the traffic and I saw my chance. I took off in a mad flurry of pedaling and headed for the middle of the road. Almost immediately there was a logging truck roaring up behind me. I could hear the driver downshifting to slow down before he pancaked me. It was huffing and puffing like a fire breathing dragon. The driver slowed so that he was mere feet behind me. I rode onto the grating and could see the river below me. It was a beautiful blue and had small sandy and rocky areas broken up by rivulets of water. I knew that one slip of the tires and I would be mashed like cheese through a grater. I could *feel* the impatience of the truck behind me. "Outa my way, I got logs to deliver." My shirt was flapping like a flag in a stiff wind. I was riding as fast as I could considering there was nothing aerodynamic about my bike. My legs hadn't burned like this since Going To The Sun Highway, and I had fleeting worries that I was going to blow out my knees again. The noise of the truck's tires on the grating was almost unbearable. I looked up and saw an outgoing logging truck coming towards me in the other lane. I instinctively moved to the right and he passed by with feet to spare. I was buffeted by its wind but stayed upright. With a hundred yards left, I saw a gravel parking area to the right and decided to head for it. The driver, sensing that I was about to bail out of his way, started to give the truck some gas and inched even closer to my rear fender. At the end of the bridge, I ran off the road and the truck passed by as I skidded to a stop in the parking lot throwing gravel every-which-a-way, miraculously upright and not squashed through the grating. As I caught my breath, I watched as each individual made his own mad dash across the bridge and came to a stop next to me wide eyed and breathing hard. Finally, Henry made it across. Trying to catch his breath, he said, in typical Henry fashion, "It's (puff, puff!) all part (wheeeeze!) of the experience."

That afternoon at the campsite we found out that Steve was leaving the trip the next morning. He had had enough and was flying back to Dallas. We would be down to seven riders: Garry, Dale, Arnold, Tim, Henry, John, and me. I was very disappointed that Steve was leaving. He had had no problems (as far as I could tell) with the ride. He had always been good-natured and never negative about anything. He was just the type of guy you would expect to be able to make a trip like this. It had been different with Tom and Pete. They were more settled in their home lives than the rest of us, and had had more professional type jobs at home. They didn't really have the stamina mentally or physically for the trip. They were both in that part of life at which it is hard to give up creature comforts for riding long days and sleeping on the ground. The rest of the guys had been on trips such as this or were in the age before comfort was paramount over experiences. I thought Steve was going to finish the ride. I really did. He simply said that the trip was too tough for him mentally; he just couldn't face getting up in the morning any more knowing that there was *x* number of miles ahead and that it would have to be ridden in the rain.

I could appreciate the frustration of riding through many days of bad weather, although I hadn't ridden as much as Steve had because of my hitchhiking. I had my own issues, though. I *did* experience plenty of bad weather and I *did* have to rehab myself from some frustrating knee problems that appeared, thankfully, to be behind me.

Prince George, named for a former Duke of Kent killed during World War II, was a bustling city of about 50,000. It sits at the crossroads of north—south Highway 97, and east-west Highway 16, also the confluence of the Nechako and Fraser Rivers. Prince George began as a fur-trading post, called Fort George. Established in 1807 by Simon Fraser, it was located in the center of the ancient homeland of the Lheidli T'Enne First Nation. Farming and other agriculture began around Fort George early in the 1900's as it became apparent that the

Grand Trunk Pacific Railway would pass near the fur-trading post. Today, it is a center of logging, mining, and oil exploration, and is a hub of transportation of Northern British Columbia.

I was greatly amazed to find a city of its size out in the middle of nowhere. Like virtually every place we visited in Canada, the people were delightfully (after my logging truck experience) friendly and inquisitive.

We were talking to one gent about our ride and he said, "So you rode in from the east, eh?

"Yep, we've ridden from Montana, actually," I said.

Well, we're glad you are riding through our city." (There was really no other way to get to our destination. But I let that slide.)

"Thank you. Prince George is beautiful (he beamed) although we had a pretty hairy welcoming ride across the bridge over the Fraser River."

He blinked. "You couldn't pay me to ride a bicycle across that bridge. I don't even like to drive across it. Those logging trucks are way too dangerous!"

Steve stayed at the campsite as we all pulled out the next day. His plane wasn't scheduled to leave until late morning, and he planned to do a few errands before going to the airport. His plane would take him to Vancouver, Los Angeles, then to Dallas. Within a couple of days he would be back in a comfortable bed, and we would still be riding north. I was now so comfortable that I wouldn't have wanted to trade places with him, and I kinda felt sorry for him.

Tim and I rode together all day to Vanderhoof, a ride of about sixty-two miles. The last forty miles were tough because they were into a headwind. They were tough for me but, apparently, not for Tim. He was a riding animal. He seemed never to shift gears and rode in a high gear on level road and uphill roads; he bored through the stiff headwind like an icebreaker clearing a frozen channel. He just kept grinding. I tucked in behind him and shamelessly drafted him like race cars draft each other.

When a race-car driver drafts the car in front he tucks in as close behind that car as possible to be able to take advantage of the aerodynamics when the first car breaks through the wind. This creates a sort of vacuum behind the first car that pulls the second car along. It also enables the second car to conserve gas because it doesn't have to work as hard to cut through the wind. Oddly, it helps the front car, too, by providing a little extra push from behind.

The same idea holds true in biking. In fact, I've read that the second biker uses only 1/2 to 2/3 the amount of energy by drafting than he would normally use while riding individually. It was a skill I had to pick up quickly if I was going to stay with Tim. I found that I could squeeze up close so that my front tire was almost touching his rear tire, and ride in much higher gears than I would have been able to do otherwise. He was a great wind block, but a few times I found it difficult to keep up and had to ask him to slow down. It took a fair amount of concentration on my part to stay so close. Our tires would be inches apart, and a few times I accidentally ran up against his rear tire and he wobbled. If he had gone down, I would have gone over the top of him. I couldn't have avoided it in time. Later in the trip, after I had fully regained my biking strength, we drafted together as a team. He would ride as the wind-break for a few miles, and I would draft. Then we would switch, and I would be the wind-break while he drafted. We could really move down the road as a team and it was great fun. For now, however, I was just trying to build strength and keep up. Tim was very accommodating and never complained about doing the hard work. I think he was basically shy and appreciated the company.

Tim and I arrived in Vanderhoof well before the others and made ourselves at home at the local strip mall while we waited. When Garry rode up, he told us that he had somehow managed to find us a place to stay indoors for the night. We had stayed indoors only a few times so far, and sleeping inside was beginning to seem exotic. There was nothing exotic, however, about our sleeping arrangements in Vanderhoof. We all thought the gymnasium, several streets off the main drag, would be similar to school gymnasiums in the States. Actually, it could charitably be described as an old Quonset-shaped military building masquerading as a gymnasium. It was a rectangular building with both ends shaped like a half circle with the flat sides on the ground. The roof line followed the semi-circular curve the length of the building on both sides, and was made of tin. There were no windows and only one door at each end. Over the years, water had rotted the plywood walls on the ends of the building so much that it appeared that one good strong wind could lift the whole thing up and send it cartwheeling across British Columbia to end in a resounding, but pleasing crash. Still, we didn't want to "look a gift horse in the mouth" and happily moved in for the night.

Arnold and I rummaged around some closets and found a softball-sized ball which we used for shooting baskets, and we also found some hockey sticks, and then we used the ball as a stand-in for a hockey puck. A comical game of gym floor hockey ensued as everyone, even Henry, took part.

As our trip continued northward, the nights were getting shorter. The sun would set about 11:30 PM and would come up at about 4:00 AM. After we closed the doors, our night in the gym was the first totally dark night that we could remember.

11

June 26–30

✦

1,264 miles from Missoula

It was agony on the eighty-three mile ride the next day to Burns Lake. There was a howling headwind all day, and it never let up. To add to the frustration, it seemed that whichever way the road turned, the wind was always in our face. Tim and I rode together again and ended up at another strip mall with the local drugstore cowboys. We figured that these guys were shift workers, worked at night, and hung around the mall during the day. Probably the same back in Vanderhoof. Our campground offered showers for $1.50. I opted to wait until the next rest day. I didn't think I smelled too bad considering, and I was developing a theory about smelly sweat. We typically ate a largely vegetarian diet partly because vegetables didn't need to be refrigerated and partly because it was cheaper to eat vegetables. I didn't think we smelled as bad after eating an all-vegetable diet. Whenever we included meat into the diet, we seemed to smell worse. My theory is that a person's sweat doesn't smell as bad when a person avoids meat. It's just a theory, and it would be interesting if someone did a study on it to see if it is actually true.

Tim was an interesting fellow to try to get to know. Very quiet and shy he was from Milwaukee. He had been on a Trans-America trip several years before and had saved up for this trip by working in a factory. He was a monster rider; he had thighs that looked like tree trunks and arms that were not much smaller. He was solidly built and he appeared to be impervious to cold. When the weather was nasty, rainy, snowy, or whatever, the others would be dressed in layers with long pants, long-sleeved shirts, wool sweaters, and Gore-Tex jackets. I was particularly wimpy; I would wear my blue jeans every day to keep my knees warm and wear my various long-sleeved shirts and jacket at the first hint of chilly weather. I went days without taking my coat off. Tim, on the other hand, would wear only gym shorts, a tee shirt, and a baseball cap. Occasionally, if the rain was particularly hard, he would put on a light nylon jacket, but mostly he just soldiered on with the minimum of clothing. He was unflappable; nothing or nobody bothered him. There was a period when he was plagued with flat tires. When he heard the tell-tale "hiiisssss" of the tire going flat, he would just say, "Well, I've got another flat tire," and get off to fix it. Once, when I was drafting too close, my front tire hit his back tire and it took a miraculous save from him to stay upright. I apologized profusely and he simply said, "Oh, it's okay." That was it. No, "Will you be a little more careful," or anything like that.

The fifty mile ride to Houston was another day of headwinds, but we had our first 24 hour day without rain since the beginning of the trip. We had had several beautiful days in a row, but some days had an occasional rain squall blow through, or it might have rained during the night. The standing joke was that when we got to a town, invariably someone would say, "We were having a drought until you guys got here."

We camped at a roadside rest area with a few picnic tables and a pit toilet. There was a stream, but the water looked polluted and we arranged to get our water from a farmhouse nearby. It was amazing what the group was able to cook up wherever we were. That night, we had chili, mashed potatoes, homemade bread, and cookies.

I noticed that we were all eating large amounts at meals. I guessed we were burning 5,000-6,000 calories every day. After I started riding full-time again, I had turned into an eating maniac. I was now fixing myself three sandwiches to take for lunch as well as apples, bananas, or granola bars. Whenever we came across a roadside café or store, I always went in for a piece of pie, milkshake, or other snack. We were riding long miles, but no one appeared to be losing weight. We were becoming efficient machines; fuel in, energy out.

Physically, I thought I was operating at about 95%. My knees were holding up well even though we were putting in a lot of time in the saddle. My last two fingers on my left hand were getting tingly and a little numb from the pressure of the way the handlebars hit the crease in my left hand. Arnold let me have an old pair of biking gloves he had, and I scavenged a piece of foam to slide inside the glove for extra cushioning. The numbness hadn't gotten any worse. I was wearing my blue jeans daily to keep my knees warm and since they were my only real pair of long pants, I was concerned I would wear the seat and knees out before the end of the trip. I hadn't counted on exclusively wearing blue jeans the whole trip.

Arnold stitching eyes back on a teddy bear he found beside the road.

A hilly 41 miles to Smithers went pretty fast. The sky clouded up and eventually turned to rain as we set up camp. Tim and I had been fortunate to come upon a deer next to the road, as well as a mother grouse with chicks. Probably the oddest part of the day was when we were riding along and I was startled to be eye-to-eye with a very agitated hummingbird. I suppose he took affront at us for having the temerity to ride through his territory, or maybe he had had one too many stiff nectars with his buddies and was over the legal limit for this part of British Columbia. Whatever. He zoomed back and forth a few times between Tim and me, flew off, and then came back for a last taunt. When we last saw him, he was bobbing and weaving towards some roadside flowers behind us.

We stopped for lunch at a picturesque little town named Telkwa, or "meeting of the waters," where the Bulkley and Telkwa Rivers meet in the heart of town. Telkwa began as the settlement, Aldemere, that was a stopping point for travelers and prospectors on the Telegraph Trail and those looking to hit it big in the Gold Rush. The town was surveyed in 1904 and offered the first hotel, general store, newspaper and post office in the Bulkley River Valley.

Getting to Telkwa was not an easy task for the first settlers. They had to travel from Prince Rupert on the coast of British Columbia to the settlement of Hazelton west of Telkwa. There were many places where settlers had to unload and walk as their boat was being winched through dangerous canyons on the Skeena River to Hazelton. It didn't get any easier after they arrived in Hazelton. Settlers had to take wagons for the remainder of the trip to Telkwa, and there were several places where they had to dismantle their wagons to be able to traverse the rougher parts of the route.

Our lunch site in Eddy Park overlooked an unusual turn in the river that caused the water to move in three directions at once. The main channel of water turned a sharp right and flowed back upstream for several hundred feet where it took a sharp left and continued its flow back downstream.

John and I were the cooks and had stopped at a grocery store in Smithers to pick up supplies. We might have chosen a different grocery store or different menu had we known what was in store for him and me the next few days. We made Sloppy Joe's, macaroni, peas, and green beans.

Sometime during the night, I sat straight up and felt as if my insides were going to boil right out. My stomach was churning, I had broken into a cold sweat. I had cramps in my lower abdomen. A jackhammer was digging through my head. I had to get out of the tent. NOW! I was zipped up in my sleeping bag and likewise zipped inside my tent. In the best of times, it took some effort to get out of the bag and the tent.

This was not the best of times.

I fumbled with the sleeping bag zipper but got it down far enough to slide out. In one lucky zip of the tent door I was out in the wet grass, in my underwear, sprinting for the nearest pit toilet.

I didn't make it.

I lost dinner.

I lost lunch.

I lost breakfast.

I started losing the previous day's meals.

I felt as if my insides would turn inside out.

After a few minutes, I felt able to get back in my tent.

In another hour or so, I had to repeat the process.

Except this time it was diarrhea.

In a pit toilet.

Instant and devastating.

Cold sweat.

Headache.

Over and over again.

Weakly climbing into my tent and back out again.

When the sun came up, I could barely get out of the tent to tell Garry and Dale that I was sick.

We had ridden about 470 miles since our last rest day in Jasper, and it was another 222 miles to our next scheduled rest day in Stewart. We were all pretty tired. Garry decided we needed the break, so he called an impromptu rest day in Smithers.

It was just as well; I couldn't have gotten on my bike, much less, ridden it any-where. All day long I was in terrible shape. When I was not *in* the toilet, I was either heading *to* or *from* the toilet. The few times I was able to actually lie down in my tent for a few minutes, the sun through the light blue tent walls actually made me nauseous, too.

I couldn't eat anything all day, but someone went to the store and brought me back a large bottle of 7-Up to try and ease my stomach. I was so weak, Henry had to open the top for me. As far as I could tell, no one else had any problems. Even-tually, I had nothing left to give the pit toilet and was able to sleep some during the rest of the day. I just ate a little ice cream for dinner as my only solid food of the day, went to bed early, and I didn't have any more "episodes" that night.

The next morning, I woke up after having slept through the night. I was feel-ing a little better although I felt as if I had been tossed around in a big mixer. I ate a little hot cereal and Garry came over and said:

"Well, at least you aren't dead."

I mumbled, "Thanks. There were times when *that* seemed preferable during the last couple of days."

"The group is going on to Hazelton. You know the drill. You can stay here for another day, you can hitchhike again, or you can ride. We are a day behind, and don't want to lose too many more days. We still have a long way to go."

I understood that the group waits for no one for long. I had to take stock of what I thought I could do.

I packed up and thought I'd ride to the main road where I would hitchhike to our next stop, Hazelton, forty-eight miles away. I was lightheaded and felt almost as if my head was disjointed from my body. When I hit the main road, I turned the bike west and to my surprise, made it the whole distance, although very slowly.

We crossed several canyons and passed through several Indian towns before we got to Hazelton. It rained on us several times and I hid in a rest-area outhouse during a particularly strong rain. Canadian campgrounds, parks, and rest areas are in the most beautiful places imaginable. The downside is that most all of them prominently feature outhouses as the hygiene of choice.

Hazelton, situated at the confluence of the Skeena and Bulkley Rivers, is located in the shadow of the rugged Roche de Boule mountain range. For centu-ries, the area has been home to the Gitxsan and Wet'suwet'en people. The town was a commercial center for the Northwest Canadian frontier in the late 1800's and early 1900's. From 1886 to 1913, Hazelton was the end of the line for stern-wheel river boats traveling to the British Columbia interior up the Skeena River from Prince Rupert. Travelers had to brave the wild rapids of the Skeena as well as a host of bank robbers, daring riverboat captains, strange mountain men, unscrupulous bankers, and the occasional hero. If they were lucky enough to arrive unscathed, they soon dispersed to farms, mines, and far-flung settlements.

I stopped at the 'Ksan Historical Village and took in the view of some of the largest Totem Poles in the world and the rebuilt Indian Village. The campground, next to the village, seemed to be the home to the largest ravens I had ever seen. They were big, but they were clever and enterprising, too. They loitered around ours and other campsites until it looked as if we weren't paying attention, and then they would try and steal anything left on a picnic table. You had to stay vigilant or else your sandwich would just disappear.

I was still feeling pretty washed out, but I thought I could continue riding the next day. John, on the other hand, was starting to feel bad. I hoped he wouldn't get the same thing I had.

The ride the next day would be about forty-five miles on Highway 16. Then we would turn due north at Kitwanga Junction, onto the gravel Stewart-Cassiar Highway, for about another forty miles to our next stop at Cranberry Junction. We would stay on the Stewart-Cassiar Highway for about 500 miles and cross into the Yukon Territory at Watson Lake. The key word here is: *gravel*.

Garry chose the gravel Stewart-Cassiar Highway as our way north instead of the more famous (and mostly paved) Alaska (Alcan) Highway because it had less traffic and offered more opportunities to see wildlife. He also said there was a certain "romance" about gravel. We planned to be on gravel roads even after we got to Yukon, so the total mileage on gravel would be about 1,300. I passed up "romance" by not going with Mary. I couldn't imagine how this would take its place.

12

July 1–2

✦

1,438 miles from Missoula

Mickey and Tim turn north up the gravel Stewart-Cassiar Highway.
The group stayed on gravel roads for nearly a month.

I was still pretty weak from being sick in Smithers. Even so, the 45 miles to Kitwanga Junction was a fairly easy ride. I had started the day with the first shower I'd had since Prince George, almost a full week, and it really made me feel better. Aside from being sick, I had enjoyed the ride from Prince George. This area of British Columbia was undeniably beautiful, and the people were very friendly. The mosquitoes, however, were becoming a major nuisance, and it was a condition that Garry said would only get worse. I couldn't see how it could be much worse. It wasn't possible to stand still for more than a few seconds to eat meals before the blood-thirsty little buggers would be all over you.

It became a race to get into my tent before the mosquitoes figured out what I was doing. I never thought of mosquitoes as having brains, but they were amazingly clever. It was important to plan my tent-entering strategy carefully so I didn't carry too many inside with me. Being zipped in with blood thirsty mosquitoes could make for a very uncomfortable and infuriating night.

Entering my tent was something like this: I would walk away from the tent just slow enough that it would cause the mosquitoes to be interested enough to follow. I hoped this would clear out some airspace for the mad dash back to my tent. Naturally, there were some clever mosquitoes that hovered near the door of the tent and rode inside while I was hustling in to keep the main horde outside.

Once inside, it was smack, smack, smack, smack, smack, to dispatch the mosquitoes that came in with me. Here is where it was good that it was still daylight at bed time. I could still see them and whack them. If it had been dark, it would have been maddening.

Tim and I arrived at Kitwanga Junction and turned right at the big sign that said, "North to Alaska," onto the Stewart-Cassiar Highway. After a few miles, the road turned to gravel. We would essentially be on gravel roads for the next 1,300 miles.

We had another forty or so miles to Cranberry Junction, our stop for the night. The road for the first twelve miles was good, but then the gravel got progressively worse so that the last twenty miles was like riding in a dry creek bed that someone had perversely called a road. There were little tiny rocks that would skitter out from under the tire with a "ping" sound. There were jagged rocks that could easily cut a tire if you weren't paying attention, and there were large, smooth rocks that looked like they had once resided at the bottom of a fast moving river. To make matters more difficult, and to add a little danger to the situation of trying to figure out how to ride in this stuff, logging trucks were zooming by us throwing rocks all around, sometimes even hitting us. It was hard enough not to get bowled over by the trucks on a paved, two-lane road. It was an extremely ticklish situation now; the trucks went by at almost the same speed as they did on the paved highway, slinging rocks, on a road that was 1/3 narrower. We had to remember that even though the road looked like a country lane, it was considered a major highway in this part of British Columbia. We would be seeing all sorts of vehicles traveling at all speeds on the gravel.

We stopped once to watch trucks being filled with logs next to the road and had to wait a few minutes until the equipment was out of the way enough for us to squeeze by. The going was tough. It took a whole different type of effort to ride on the gravel. Rocks could throw you off the road; wheels could slide, making you lose traction; potholes were sometimes hidden under dust and you wouldn't even know they were there until you hit one; trucks and buses really threw off a lot of dust, which just covered us when they went by; and there were bumpy sections of the road, like a washboard, where vehicles had torn up the road.

By the time we arrived at Cranberry Junction, we had ridden 85 miles in 9 ½ hours. After the turnoff at Kitwanga Junction, the day turned into a real grind. To make matters worse, it started raining just as we set up our tents. Our campsite at Cranberry Junction can best be described as "a large, gravel-filled area next to a stream." There was no level area to comfortably set up a tent and there were no picnic tables or even pit toilets. But there were mosquitoes. Many mosquitoes. Lots and lots of nasty little mosquitoes that probably had fantasy dreams every night of a smorgasbord of campers at their little gravel campground. Apparently, they hadn't seen warm-blooded creatures for a long time because they were relentless. They would swarm around our heads like angry bees as we swatted at them. None of us had brought bug repellant, which was looking like a really bad oversight. Arnold was the only one of the group with foresight to bring a hat with mosquito netting. Even he was cussing as one or two got inside the net and buzzed around his face.

We normally shopped for groceries at various towns as we passed through. A few times we had to carry store-bought food as far as twenty miles before getting to our stopping place for the night. For this part of the trip, Garry knew there were no grocery stores for 60 miles one way and about 85 miles in the other direction. We had pre-shipped freeze-dried food to the Hazelton post office so we would have food for this part of the trip without having to worry about it going bad.

Garry fixed up some gummy noodles, and we had some freeze-dried ice cream that tasted about as good as flavored cardboard. Garry also brought along a bottle of white and a bottle of red wine to celebrate the first day on gravel. It was raining and getting colder, so everyone took a perfunctory sip and headed for their tents to battle the mosquitoes before going to bed.

Miserable! That's about all I can say for the eighty-nine mile ride to Stewart. It rained all night and was still raining as we took our tents down. It was always a nasty task to fold up wet tents and to put them on our bikes. I learned to take all the hardware (poles, tent stakes) out while leaving the waterproof tent fly covering the rest of the tent until the last minute. Then I would quickly fold it and the bottom part of the tent and stuff them into the tent stuff sack. A dry tent weighed about 7 ½ pounds, and a wet one probably weighed 9 or 10 pounds. Those extra pounds from a wet tent as well as wet panniers added up to having to use more energy during the ride. Pounds really mattered.

We hurriedly ate some sort of freeze-dried breakfast (not sure what it was, exactly) and left Cranberry Junction. It was cold and pouring rain all morning. The clouds were low, with fog hovering in the dark evergreen trees lining the road. We did, unexpectedly, get on some pavement for about forty-five miles, and the going was pretty fast until about three miles from Meziadin Junction, when the road turned to gravel again and became steeper and rougher. The gravel road had turned into this soupy kind of gray mud and cars and trucks had splashed us with water, mud, or both all morning. I was wearing most of my clothes because it was one of those types of cold that chills you to the bone, and I had my green Gore-Tex rain pants and jacket on. My shoes and wool gloves were soaked through with cold rain. It was cold enough to see your breath.

I had started off from Cranberry Junction feeling reasonably rested, but when Tim and I arrived at Meziadin Junction, I was exhausted. I had ridden about 186 miles in two and a half days, after having been sick as a dog in Smithers. We planned to ride another 36 miles to Stewart, B.C., for our next rest stop and I wasn't sure if I was going to make it. I had a curious mixture of the shakes because I still hadn't been able to eat as much as I needed, and a creeping sort of frustration at the weather that was bordering on seething anger.

Tim and I stopped for lunch in the little café at the junction, where there were hundreds of Canadian and American dollars stapled to the walls and ceiling as a kind of monetary graffiti. Normally, after a good slice of pie I would think this was interesting. This day, that wasn't going to work. I was weak, tired, cranky, wet, muddy, and, today, I was *really, really,* sorry I hadn't left the trip with Pete, Tom, and Steve.

I told Tim to go on and I would meet him in Stewart because I needed to go slow and pace myself. He disappeared into the mist hanging low over the road, and I plodded on towards Stewart. The Stewart-Cassiar Highway basically runs north-south from Kitwanga Junction to where it joins the Alaska Highway just outside of Watson Lake, Yukon. At Meziadin Junction, instead of continuing north, we took a road west towards Stewart. It is the only road that goes to Stewart, and we would have to backtrack to Meziadin Junction before turning north again on the Stewart-Cassiar Highway.

I'm certain the road between Meziadin Junction and Stewart had spectacular scenery; you knew it was there even if you couldn't always see it.

I didn't care.

I didn't want to be there.

I wanted to be anywhere else but there.

If anyone had come along and offered me a job as a javelin catcher in a warm dry place, I would have taken it.

I looked down and the road was a soaking gray slop.

I looked up and the sky was the same color as the road.

The world had turned gray.

My bike had turned gray.

My panniers had turned gray.

My green rain pants and jacket had also turned gray.

Everything on my bike was soaked.

Cold rain trickled off the back of my helmet, under my hood and down my back.

Water skooshed up through the mesh of my shoes.

When a truck sloshed by and covered me with another layer of mud, I lost it.

I mean I *really* lost it.

I had had enough. I was tired of the rain, the mud, the cold, and the scenery that I couldn't see. I was sick and tired of being sick and tired.

I did what seemed appropriate; I threw a good, old-fashioned temper tantrum.

I started yelling. Nothing specific, just yelling.

Then I started screaming. The sound was coming from deep within. The frustrations of knees with tendonitis and the stomach virus were venting like a volcano about ready to explode.

Then, I started cussing. First, one word, then another, then more gushed out of me like water from a fire hydrant. After a while, I started stringing cuss words together into phrases.

@%&*!!! @#$$*&%!!! @#$%&*@#$%&*@#$%&*!!! @#%#$*&@#+$*!!!

I had turned into a wet and gray wild man. Some people in a car slowed to look at me and sped off when I gave them a crazy-eyed look. My bike weaved all over the road as I spewed invectives.

I cussed the road.

I cussed the weather.

I cussed myself for cussing.

I'm really not sure how long this tirade went on. Two miles? Five miles?

My mouth was frothing. My voice was getting scratchy from screaming. I was sweating from the exertion of venting my frustrations.

And, suddenly, it was over.

Breathing hard, I got off my bike and immediately felt absolute calm and peace. It was amazing! One minute I was borderline bonkers; the next minute I was the happiest, most laid back guy in British Columbia. I had had a big-time cathartic moment.

My attitude had finally turned the corner. I suppose there was still some bad attitude that was being held back by my subconscious, but it was blasted out in my crazy spell. Now, I felt like nothing could bother me for the rest of the trip.

You wanna rain on me? Hah! Hit me with your best shot!

Mud? Trivial.

Mosquitoes? Ah, well, they were still going to tick me off.

Anyway, I stood in the rain in my muddy clothes, with rain dripping down my neck, and just started laughing. Now, anyone that drove by would be thinking that that guy, covered in gray mud, standing out in the rain, laughing his head off, is loony. I didn't care. I had experienced a cathartic moment, and all was well.

The rest of the ride into Stewart was fun, mostly downhill, and as an added bonus, the rain stopped.

13

July 3–5

✦

1,474 miles from Missoula

Stewart, BC, is located at the head of the Portland Canal, a narrow fjord that leads about 90 miles to the Pacific Ocean. The canal forms a natural boundary between British Columbia and Alaska and borders the rugged Alaska Misty Fjords National Park. The Nass River Indians hunted the area and called it "Skam-a-Kounst," meaning "safe place" a refuge from the aggressive coastal Hiadas Indians. A settlement sprang up as a mining community when 68 miners looking for gold came up the Portland Canal to stake a claim they hoped would equal the Klondike Gold Rush. Although these miners didn't hit it big, they were the backbone for the beginnings of very successful gold, silver, and copper mining in the area. In 1902, the Stewart brothers arrived and promptly named the little settlement after themselves.

Stewart is slightly known for being the northernmost ice-free port on the west coast of Canada, but its real claim to fame is the amazing amount of snow that buries it during the long, dark winter. As I rode into town, I started noticing many houses that had a door on the ground floor on one end of the house and a door on the second floor that seemingly opened into thin air on the other end. A sleepwalking person opening the door on the second floor would resemble Wile E. Coyote stepping off a cliff before plummeting headlong to the ground. When I asked a townsperson about the strange doors she gave a rueful chuckle and said that is the door they enter and exit during the winter when snow reaches the second floor.

Oh.

It had started raining again, and I took quick refuge in a building that turned out to be the Stewart Museum. It was in an old, two-story building and didn't look like it was overrun with visitors. In fact, the lady at the desk was so happy to have a visitor that she personally took me around the museum on an impromptu guided tour.

"Here is our room dedicated to drill-bits," she said with obvious pride.

"I see. These look like very nice drill-bits"

"Thank you. It's the most complete collection in this part of British Columbia. She leaned toward me and confidentially whispered as her eyes suspiciously darted from side to side: "There are several other museums that covet our drill bit collection."

"Really?"

"Oh yes, you would never imagine how competitive museums can get over exhibits."

"I never knew."

And so it went from room to room through exhibits of turn of the century clothing, furniture, and more mining relics.

The docent was particularly enthusiastic about showing me the exhibit from the Hollywood movie, called "Bear Island," that had recently been filmed there.

"Over here is the movie poster."

"Uh, huh. It's a nice poster."

"And here is a hat that Lloyd wore."

"Lloyd?"

"Bridges. Surely you remember him from TV."

"Of course. He was the scuba guy."

"Right. And here is a cup used by Vanessa."

"Vanessa?"

"Redgrave."

"Oh, and here is a picture of Donald." (She seemed to know all the stars on a first name basis.)

"O'Connor?"

"No. Sutherland." She narrowed her eyes. "You haven't seen the movie, have you?"

"Well…no."

"I thought Americans went to movies all the time."

"Ah, well, I, uh, just finished graduate school, you see. I've been studying pretty hard for a couple of months. Did the movie just come out?"

Somewhat disgustedly she said, "Over a year ago." She seemed incredulous that I had managed to miss Stewart's fifteen minutes of fame.

Vicar Sheila, and her friend Josi, in front of Sheila's house in Stewart, BC.

Garry, the guru of finding places to spend the night indoors, had finagled a place to stay at the parsonage of the acting vicar of the local Anglican Church, Sheila Green. Sheila graciously opened the second floor of the parsonage to us and good naturedly watched as we all dragged wet and dirty panniers and clothes into her house. I think she was glad to have company, even though it was a bunch of grizzly looking bikers. And we were happy to have a warm place out of the rain with a kitchen and laundry.

All of us were in Stewart except John. The last anyone saw of him, he was feeling really sick and trying to hitchhike his way to Stewart. We guessed that whatever I had had finally caught up with him. We kept an eye out for him all night, but he never showed up at Sheila's.

The next day, July 3, was spent catching up on laundry and sleeping. Garry called the local RCMP headquarters to inquire if they had seen John anywhere along the road from Meziadin Lake to Stewart. They hadn't, but promised to keep a lookout during their patrols up and down the road.

The southeast Alaska town of Hyder was a mile away from Stewart, just around the curve of the Portland Canal. Garry and I rode over to mail some letters and to poke around the settlement.

Hyder, Alaska, has maybe fifty inhabitants, and is reachable only by boat or by the road through Stewart, which is on a side road of the Stewart-Cassiar Highway in British Columbia. So, if Stewart is remote, Hyder is more so.

As far as I could gather, Hyder's real claim to fame came from the drinking term "Getting Hyderized," which involves large amounts of liquor with a water chaser. The town was named Portland (after the canal) until the United States Post Office informed townsfolk that there were already too many towns named Portland in the U.S. It is also the gateway to several gold mines located in the mountains behind the town.

Garry became more worried about John and decided to hitchhike back to Meziadin Junction to try and find him. Once he got there, he found John at the campground being tended to by a couple of other campers. John had been so sick that he been retching for miles. He started getting chills so bad that he had had to pull off the road at some point during the ride to Meziadin Lake from Cranberry Junction and crawl into his sleeping bag in the woods off the road. After warming up in the sleeping bag he had just enough strength to ride to Meziadin Junction. He apparently looked so bad that several campers immediately put him to bed and considered calling a doctor. When Garry arrived, he had recovered enough to travel to Stewart. Garry then hitched back to Stewart and persuaded Sheila to drive back with him to Meziadin to pick up John. When John got to Sheila's house he looked like death warmed over and went straight to bed near the upstairs bathroom.

As he did when I was sick, Garry called an impromptu rest day for the next day to give John extra time to recuperate. I can't say that any one of us was disappointed to spend an extra day in the warmth and conviviality of Sheila's house, and truth be told, she seemed fond of us. She received an added benefit of some really great meals that we cooked, and we cleaned her house top to bottom. We took turns walking her big dog, "King," and even he seemed delighted with all the attention.

Even with a house full of bikers, she still needed to perform her ministerial duties. As soon Garry and she returned with John, she hurried over to her church for an evening prayer meeting. She was kind enough to invite any of us who wanted to come, and Arnold, Henry, and I took her up on it. The church was very small, built to seat no more than fifty people. It was painted white with green trim around the door and windows. It had an English type garden with a welcoming riot of flowers on either side of the front steps. Inside, the church was rustic, yet full of warmth. The pews had that solid feel of having been there for ages. The floor was agreeably creaky. The simple lighting set a proper reverential mood. A sign with replaceable letters was located on the wall next to the pulpit and had page numbers for the hymns as well as the past Sunday's attendance, which was 23. The parishioners showed great interest in us and treated us with the utmost respect. Because of the remoteness of their town, they understood better than most what an effort it took for us to be able to be with them at the prayer service in Stewart. Kids wanted to sit with us in the pews. Afterwards, when everyone had adjourned to the front yard for after-church conversation, the kids begged us to swing them around and around in big circle, which we did until we were giddy with dizziness.

I had moved my sleeping bag from upstairs down to the couch in the living room because I didn't want to be pinned into a little room with a bunch of snoring guys, or with John who was still an invalid near the upstairs bathroom. Sometime during the night, I thought I had a dream in which I was sleeping out in the open and it had started raining. At least I thought it was raining because my face sure felt like it was getting wet. When I opened my eyes I was startled to see King, the dog, looking playfully at me. My face was covered in dog slobber where he had been licking me.

It was about the time we were in Stewart that I noticed my appetite was continuing to grow. I know this because I ate six pieces of French toast for breakfast on the Fourth of July. A friend of Sheila's, a lady named Josi, offered to take several of us sightseeing to the abandoned Premiere Gold Mine in the mountains outside of Hyder. Sheila, Garry, Dale, Josi, and her two kids, and I jumped into the back of her car for a harrowing ride up some very steep and narrow roads to the gold mine. The scenery was alpine looking with beautiful snow capped peaks. There was not much to be seen at the mine. Actually the trip up and back was more interesting than the destination. Several times on the way back down the car skidded on loose gravel and it seemed to me we were perilously close to being launched into space. Josi didn't seem to notice that we were skittering on the brink and kept up a running commentary about the gold mines, the scenery, and church business with Sheila.

We treated Sheila to a big breakfast and a final whirlwind clean up of her house before we headed back out the road to Meziadin the next day. It was Sunday, and we all visited Sheila's church for the morning service. We regretted leaving the friendly confines of Sheila's house and Stewart, but we had to keep riding.

We left after lunch, and it occurred to me that we had been spoiled for three days and had been living the soft life. Now we were heading back to days of hard riding and hard ground. Just to remind us of what we had been missing, it started raining. We had to leave John at Sheila's. He was slowly recovering but had slept through church and would catch up with us by hitchhiking later.

The thirty-six mile ride to Meziadin Lake was easy and I got to see what I had missed during my ranting and raving spell on the way in to Stewart. We were riding up a very beautiful alpine valley with mountains rising steeply from both sides of the road. There were hundreds of small waterfalls tumbling down the mountains from the snowcapped peaks. We saw a black bear foraging near the road, as well as several bald eagles gliding overhead. As far as I knew, this was the first time I had ever seen bald eagles in the wild, and it was a magnificent experi-ence. One flew by so low that it was actually possible to hear its feathers flapping in the wind. Shortly after seeing the eagles, we came upon the great Bear Glacier which flows from the Cambria Icefield and stops several hundred yards short of the road. The ice was a brilliant blue, even more so than at the Athabasca Glacier, and the closest approximation of color would be Carolina Blue. It was hard to imagine that something as large as the Bear Glacier could have been missed by me on my ride into Stewart. As I said, the weather, and my attitude, was really bad…

John finally caught up with us at Meziadin Lake and looked ready to ride. He searched for the campers that had taken care of him to give them his thanks, but unfortunately they had moved on.

14

July 6–9

✦

1,687 miles from Missoula

The trip to our next stop, Hodder Lake, was fifty-eight miles of eating dust from the logging trucks. We were also carrying all our food for the next three days since there would be no towns in which to buy groceries. It looked as if we had to look forward to three days of freeze dried noodles, stroganoff, and cardboard ice cream.

Yummy!

Poster board with syrup actually would have tasted better, and was probably as nutritious, but it was too bulky to carry.

During the ride, Tim, Garry, Dale, and I saw a moose wandering aimlessly in the road in front of us. We stopped, waiting for it to go into the woods. It stopped too, and looked at us. It had a huge rack of antlers and we could hear it breathing. It took a few steps toward us and we were about to do a jailbreak the other way when it stopped again and walked placidly off the road. We watched to make sure it was far enough in the woods for us to quickly ride by, and we wasted no time putting distance between us.

The mosquitoes and black flies were just obnoxious at Hodder Lake. We had decided to take a dip in the lake to take the dust off and when they sensed our presence, they were out for our blood. A quick dip was torment as both swarmed around us and started feasting on our exposed flesh. The mosquitoes were bad, but there was no comparison to the crazed black fly. The mosquitoes would go for your arms and legs while the black flies would suddenly materialize in a huge swarm around your head, and actually seemed as if they were all trying to land on your eyeball at the same time. When they missed, they would come around again for another go. Or, if they were feeling a little extra daring, they would just fly right into your ear and rattle around in there like a pebble in a garbage can. We had little defense. We slathered up with bug lotion we had purchased in Stewart, and our long sleeves and scraggly beards provided some protection. Any other exposed areas would end up with big welts.

We spent the better part of dinner walking around while madly swatting at anything that buzzed by. We were all so preoccupied with walking and swatting that no one noticed the really large black bear that had parked itself just across the road to watch the excitement. Arnold was the first to notice it, and his eyes got really large, and his mouth opened, and it was moving like he was trying to say something, but nothing was coming out. We all stopped and followed his gaze to the bear that was now pacing back and forth not more than fifty feet from us. We were all momentarily frozen with surprise with no real plan of action going forward. Suddenly, from the direction we had just ridden, a car pulled into the rest area playing loud music. The driver slid to a stop and never saw the bear 20 feet away from him. The bear apparently didn't like Kenny Rogers music because he bolted off into the woods and we didn't see him any more. The small rest area quickly filled with other travelers coming in from the way we were going and from the way in which we came.

Amazingly, the rest area became sort of like a fraternity party and started rocking. The Kenny Rogers man had plenty of other selections, and fired up his car stereo. Someone said they had lawn chairs, others had food and drink. I swear, it was as if the party had been planned in advance with all participants receiving assignments on what to bring. We couldn't offer much in the way of food to the party; no one was interested in our pitiful assortment of freeze dried foods, but we were celebrities anyway. Everyone wanted to talk about our trip, check out our equipment, and tell their own bike stories. When someone told a bike story, it was always a tale of flat tires or bikes being run over by steam rollers. Anything to make a connection with us seemed fair game. It was apparent that these people would be spending the night all jammed together with us at the Hodder Creek rest area. We were glad of course, there was safety in numbers just in case Mr. Bear came back, but it also meant that we would probably get little sleep in the midst of an impromptu Rush Party. An added benefit for us was that the black flies and mosquitoes left us and went to the greener pastures of car and RV passengers. Some of which had already started swatting at them.

As I climbed unmolested into my tent, I watched entranced as a pasty, heavy set woman from an RV became the center of attention of hordes of mosquitoes and black flies. She was wearing shorts and a way-too-tight top with spaghetti straps. And she must have been wearing some sort of lotion or perfume that attracted them because the bugs were in a frenzy to get at her ample skin. Initially, she casually swatted around her head. Then, alarmed, she started jogging around the gravel rest area madly flapping her arms in a display that would have impressed a lovesick albatross. Around and around the rest area she went in her flimsy, high-heeled sandals. She stopped and tried a quick change of direction whereupon she broke a sandal strap and lost her right sandal. By now, everyone was watching. Hopping and yelping, she charged by my tent. I could definitely feel the wind as she went by and fancied that I could hear the evil buzzing of hundreds of bugs following her. Her good sandal was now starting to flap and make the sound of a flat tire. She juked around the Kenny Rogers man, who had the look of a deer caught in headlights at the possibility of being bowled over, and headed for her RV. She was about halfway there when her other sandal ejected from her foot and, at the same time, one of the straps holding her top broke. She covered the last few yards with amazing speed for someone her size while flapping one arm at the bugs and using the other to hold up her top. She fumbled with the door to the RV, and it was open long enough to let in an unknown number of mosquitoes and black flies. We could hear cursing and crashes inside the RV, and her shouting to her husband to start the "damn RV, and let's get the hell out of here." He floored the gas pedal and they sprayed gravel all around the rest area as they careened south and away from Hodder Lake.

The next day, Tim was very lucky on the sixty-eight mile ride to Eastman Creek. We had been riding on some of the best dirt roads so far, and were confidently going about twenty-five to thirty miles an hour down a hill when suddenly, and very unexpectedly, we hit some very thick, loose gravel. I was able to skirt around the edge and slow down, but Tim hit it dead center and his bike fish-tailed several times as he tried to recover. Then, in scary slow motion, he went over the handlebars of his bike into a cartwheel. Through the dust and gravel I could see Tim and his bike tumbling together like a mad snowball in a cartoon where legs and arms are sticking out. Tim and his bike rolled for maybe twenty feet. When the dust settled, he was lying dazed under his bike, its wheels still spinning. He had ripped his sweater and had a six inch cut on top of his head, which was oozing blood (He didn't have a helmet). I jumped off my bike and ran over to him just as he wobbled to his feet, and helped him to the side of the road, where he sat down. At about that time, two road trucks came by (we had them to thank for the new gravel) and stopped when they saw the bike still in the middle of the road. The foreman kindly offered to help and took Tim and his bike to their camp just up the road. Luckily, they had a medic available who was able to put about twenty stitches in Tim's head. They even gave him a ride the rest of the way to Eastman Creek where Henry, a former paramedic, cleaned him up even more.

For the next several days, Tim rode with his head covered with a large bandage that always drew stares and comments from whomever we met. As I was finishing the ride to Eastman Creek by myself, I was riding through a dark tunnel of evergreen trees that seemed to grow out of the edges of the road, when out of the corner of my eye I noticed some movement to my left, and was startled to see what looked like a really big dog coming out of the woods on an intersecting path with me. I was even more surprised when I realized it was a wolf and not a dog. He hadn't heard me coming, and as he turned his head he was just as surprised to see me as I was him. He was large, maybe 110 pounds, with a dark gray color. He looked me square in the eye, and I saw that he had yellowish eyes and big teeth. He quickly trotted across the road ahead of me and went into the woods, watching me warily over his shoulder. I jumped on my pedals and made myself scarce. Adrenaline kicked in immediately, and I rode hard for a couple of miles before I slowed down. Only then did I realize how utterly cool and potentially dangerous our encounter had been. The wolf could have been looking for his next meal, or he could have been running with a pack of wolves looking for a nice snack. "Look guys, dinner delivered itself tonight! Whoo, hoo!" My biking buddies would have come across a bunch of satiated wolves with toothpicks and floss.

The next day, July 8, we had a relatively easy twenty-eight mile ride to the little settlement of Tatogga Lake, where we were able to take showers and have a piece of homemade pie. Both of these little actions always brightened a day of riding. Showers, especially, were very much appreciated by us and, I'm sure, the people around us.

It was another eight miles to the Indian village of Iskut, where we loaded groceries onto our bikes for another seven mile ride to our stopping point at 40 Mile Flats. The road had turned upward as we left Tatogga Lake and four of the last seven miles were uphill. We were now camping at 3,500 feet in temperatures of about 38–40F. All of us had on as many layers as possible because there was a howling wind coming from the direction we were riding the next day, and we all climbed into our tents to warm up.

Earlier, at the village of Iskut, we caused something of a sensation because the townsfolk had apparently never seen this many bikers at one time before. At the time, bike touring was still a novelty in populated areas. A group of bikers our size must have seemed unimaginably exotic to the locals who probably hadn't done much traveling. Almost a dozen little boys and girls came running as soon as we arrived, and soon they were joined by adults, who seemed curious, too. In no time at all there was a large crowd milling about that seemed to be enjoying the spectacle. Most adults asked the usual questions of how far, etc, etc. The little kids seemed only to want to touch our bikes and to hang around with someone from "outside." It was unlikely that these kids would get much opportunity to travel far away from Iskut, and it seemed they wanted to soak up our experiences by some sort of cosmic osmosis. We were instant good guys when we started offering the kids some candy bars and trail mix. After about thirty minutes, we had to ride on northward and the kids and adults headed off, the entertainment over.

We woke up to a brilliantly sunny 31F morning, on July 9. There was frost on the tents and we broke camp quickly in order to start riding and generate some heat. We continued toward an elevation of 4,000 feet at Gnat Pass, but on the way we had to cross the Stikine River.

The "Great River," as the Stikine is called, is part of the 536,229-acre Stikine River Provincial Park. The river drains nearly 20,000 square miles of Canadian and Alaskan wilderness and is the fastest free-flowing river in North America that is still navigable. The river is essentially divided into two parts: the Upper River and the Lower River. The Upper Stikine River is known for its unparalleled boating and fishing. The Lower Stikine River is highlighted by the Grand Canyon of the Stikine, a geological feature that is unusual for Canada.

The Stikine River tumbles through its fifty mile long Grand Canyon in places as much as 650 feet wide and then blasts through spots as narrow as 6 ½ feet wide. The canyon walls are 984 feet high in places and this part of the river is considered unnavigable. In fact, the canyon can be seen only from the air, since there are no roads or trails leading to it.

The ride wasn't especially long, at forty-four miles, but the gravel was thick and loose in places which clogged my derailleur and pulleys with dry mud. About every two miles the clog would make the riding so difficult that I had to get off and clean them out with a stick. Eventually, the gravel turned to hard dirt and we started descending on a wonderful downhill to the bridge crossing the Stikine River. At the bridge we were confronted with the view of the long, switchback-laden road out of the valley. Little did we know that it was the beginning of a fifteen mile climb to Gnat Pass. The thick gravel was really tough to ride through, and caused my knees to get tender even though I was riding in low gears.

The ride to Gnat Pass was a grind, and all I could do was put my head down and pedal. The scenery was loaded with beautiful forests and snow covered peaks that would be temporarily obliterated when a truck, bus, or car passed, sucking along a huge dust cloud behind it.

We made it to the top of the pass to the most glorious view we'd seen in days. We were at 4,000 feet, and the sun was sharp, and the air crisp. The mountains surrounding the pass were snow-topped. Off in the distance we could see our destination, Dease Lake, lying like a blue scarf in what looked like a welcoming valley. Again, the gravel was thick through the pass, but the downhill into Dease Lake was worth the grinding climb out of the Stikine River Valley.

Looks were deceiving when we arrived in Dease Lake. The town was nothing more than a few dusty, run-down shops, and our campsite for the night was the infield of the Dease Lake community baseball field, which had to be the dustiest place in this dusty little town.

The night before, the weather had been in the low 30's, and we had bundled up and climbed into our tents in order to get warm inside our sleeping bags. Now, in the approximate location of 2nd base, on Dease Lake's dusty baseball field, it was about 80 degrees. Normally, we would have been very happy at this good weather. Now it was working against us because the mosquitoes were swarming and it was too hot to get inside our tents or to wear long sleeves and pants to ward them off. We adjourned to a little café to escape from the pesky varmints.

15

July 10–12

◆

1,860 miles from Missoula

Fifty-four miles up the road from the dusty burg of Dease Lake was the beautifully serene Mighty Moe's campground, our next stop. The campground, located on the edge of lovely Cotton Lake, was nestled in a forest of evergreen trees down a dirt road. Months before, when I received the trip itinerary, I was looking over the listing of camping areas where we were planning to stop, and the one that said "Mighty Moe" stood out. Where virtually all listings were geographically oriented names like "Waterton" or "Purden Lake," this listing appeared to be about a person more than a place. I had been looking forward to seeing Mighty Moe's all trip.

Mighty Moe at his campground in northern Britsh Columbia.

I found out about Mighty Moe as soon as I rode into the campground. I pulled up to the main lodge, which was a small log cabin, and out walked Mighty Moe. Now, you'd think someone with the sobriquet "Mighty" in front of his name would actually be a hulking former professional wrestler. To my surprise, Mighty Moe was about 5 '4 " and 120 pounds, and he was dressed like a cowboy from a bad spaghetti western. He was wearing a black cowboy hat, a black shirt with a matching neckerchief, a tan vest and a pair of pants that had seen many miles. Oddly, he didn't complete his cowboy wardrobe with cowboy boots; he had on slippers like you would wear scuffing around the house before bedtime.

His lodge had all manner of paraphernalia hanging on the outside walls: moose antlers, various animal traps, hubcaps, license plates from assorted states and Canadian Provinces, steer horns, shovels, and one of those lawn chairs that have the aluminum tubing and nylon mesh seat and back. Inside, it was dark and cool with the main decorative feature being an old Coca-Cola cooler in the corner. Moe appeared to be selling anything from peanut butter crackers to postcards that had "I stayed with Mighty Moe in British Columbia" on the front. A pot bellied stove stood in the center of the room and looked as if it had been used for many winters. The inside walls were covered with baseball caps, lapel buttons, dollar bills, plaques, and business cards. On his desk was a large jar of ash from the recent eruption of Mt. St. Helens.

Behind the lodge was a two-story cache, also made of logs, where he kept his food safe from the bears and other animals. It was reached by a ladder propped against the side. As was the lodge, it was covered with detritus. There were snowshoes, crutches, several pairs of boots, more license plates, and a few animal skins.

In my opinion, the crowning glory of the campground, other than Moe himself, was the outdoor shower that was situated next to Cotton Lake, a short walk from the lodge. Moe looked me over and said, "I'll bet you'd really enjoy a shower."

"I sure would," I said.

"Let me show you my pride and joy."

Down the path we walked to what had to be the funniest "Rube Goldberg" contraption for travelers in British Columbia.

The "shower" was literally outdoors. It had four walls that started at about your knees and went up so that your body would be covered from knees to head. It looked very much like a stall in an overused public restroom, only not as nice. The door was held shut by a skinny piece of string looped over a nail. The hot water came from a makeshift boiler attached to the shower walls by a series of rickety looking pipes and hoses. The showerer would be standing on a box covered by old red carpet. The inside of the shower had some jerry-rigged levers to turn the water off and on, and the nozzle appeared to be hand-made from leftover scrap metal. Outside, on the wall, was handwritten lettering that said:

SHOWER
$2.00
PER, CAMPER

Naively, I asked, "How does the water get hot?"

"Why, you use the wood over there to build a fire."

I followed his gaze and saw a stack of wood several feet away.

"So, you're saying I need to pay two dollars for the shower and build my own fire to heat the water?"

"Yep. The matches and paper to start the fire are included in the cost," he added helpfully.

Well, I really needed a shower, especially after the dust bowl of Dease Lake, so I decided to give it a try. If nothing else it would give me a story for the grand-kids. I quickly put up my tent and got soap, shampoo, towel, and a change of clothes.

We carried the wood and put it in a little swale under the boiler. Good to his word, Moe appeared with newspaper and matches. I lit the fire and nursed it along until it was going pretty well. About this time Moe had to go and take care of some new campers that had just arrived, and I was left on my own to figure out how the shower worked.

When I guessed the water to be warm enough, I climbed in and pulled the door closed. I quickly took my clothes off, before the mosquitoes figured out that there was an afternoon snack over at the shower.

I turned on the lever painted red, and out came steaming hot water, which hit my leg. Startled, I jumped back, crashed into the door, which came open, and fell out onto the ground, naked as a jaybird. I hopped up, and climbed back into the shower just in time (I thought I did, anyway) to miss Mighty Moe giving the new arrivals a tour of his shower contraption. I could hear them outside discussing how the shower worked, while I busily soaped up. It apparently never occurred to Moe the awkwardness of the situation of showering in a flimsy stall while listen-ing to strangers talk just outside the door.

I heard the lady saying, "So I have to pay two dollars for the shower, and build my own fire to heat the water? Only an idiot would do that!"

"Well, the matches and paper to start the fire are free," said Moe. I could hear them muttering as they headed back toward the lodge.

The mosquitoes had discovered my spot, my privacy had been compromised, and my intellect questioned, so I quickly finished the shower and got dressed. I sheepishly opened the door and peeked outside. Moe and the campers were nowhere to be seen. No one else used the shower that afternoon, or that night.

Most preferred to take a swim in the lake, instead of taking the time to build a fire to heat the water.

The mosquitoes at Mighty Moe's were magnificent as far as mosquitoes go. They congregated between my tent fly and the inner roof of my tent, and buzzed like tiny little motors. The buzzing was as annoying as a fingernail on blackboard. "Zeeeeeee!" They also liked to gather on the screen door of my tent in hopes of getting a free ride into the tent when I came and went. It wasn't long before I made up a game where I took perverse enjoyment in putting my hand close to the screen and watching them agitatedly poke their needle-like snouts through the holes while trying get at my hand. It's really funny how you can tease mosquitoes into a frenzy. "Zeeeeee!" I could imagine their beady little eyes looking at me like I was the bloodmobile, and that they were about hit the big time. Just when the snouts were close, I pulled my hand away. "Zeeeee, zeeeee!" Delicious! When there were enough mosquitoes on the screen, I would whack it with my hand and send them tumbling into space. This happened over and over. I really had been gone too long.

It is one month to Anchorage!

The forty-five mile ride to Boya Lake was one of the most pleasant rides of the whole trip. I left Mighty Moe's at 8:15 AM. He never mentioned the shower incident as I said goodbye on the way out; I'm sure he didn't want to curtail his lucrative shower business by indiscreetly mentioning my shower mishap-if he actually saw it.

My bike in front of Good Hope Lake in northern BC.

For lunch, I stopped at a beautiful over look at Good Hope Lake. The air temperature was about 80F with a nice breeze that kept the mosquitoes away. I arrived at Boya Lake at about 1:15 PM, and decided that I would use the time waiting for the others to rotate my tires. By the time I reached Boya Lake I had worn through two tires and was on my second set. The rear tire, carrying most of the weight, got smooth faster than the tire on the front. I shifted the back tire to the front and the front to the back hoping that would last several hundred more miles. Mechanically, I was in good shape, too. I hadn't experienced any broken spokes or other major bike problem. Arnold and John had both had about ten flat tires each by the time they reached Boya Lake. So I was having much better luck than they were. I did, however, notice that a weld on my rear rack had broken from the hard wear of the gravel roads. I would need to try to get it re-welded when we arrived in Watson Lake.

Boya Lake was easily one of my favorite stops of the whole trip. There was the harmonic convergence of warm sunny weather, a breeze strong enough to keep the mosquitoes away, and a lake that was absolutely meant for swimming and sunning. The lake was shallow with a sandy bottom that gave the water the color of bright turquoise. It was also crystal clear. There was a nice dock on which to sit and get a little sun, have a little swim, and get a little more sun. No mosquitoes! Across the lake, the mountains were treeless and had a little leftover snow in the top. There were no clouds to be seen anywhere. We probably sat on the dock for two, three hours. I looked over once and Henry had his soap and shampoo and was taking a bath at the waters edge. After our experience at Purden Lake he kept his swim trunks on. We had had thirty-one days with some sort of inclement weather, but today made up for most of it. It would take several days like this in a row to make up for the ride to Stewart in the gray muddy slop.

Several of our group tried to go grocery shopping in the town of Cassiar. There was some sort of strike in town and the store was closed. They could come up with only a bag of potatoes, and we had some kind of potato dish and a trout that another camper gave us. Tim was very late for dinner because he had forgotten some of his camera accessories beside the road. He hitchhiked twenty-five miles back below Mighty Moe's and ended up riding through the heat of the day. He got into soft tar on the road and had another flat tire. He ended up riding sixty-eight to seventy miles where the rest of us rode forty-five or so.

The next day we would leave British Columbia and ride into the Yukon Territory for a rest day in Watson Lake.

We left Boya Lake at about 8:15 AM and rode for about thirty-five miles on some pretty good road. We crossed a creek and a sign said, "Narrow winding road next 19 miles." The gravel was really bad, almost like the ride into Cranberry Junction. It had large and small chunks that were sharp. One hill was so steep that I had to push my bike up it because even when I stood up to pedal, my body weight wouldn't move the pedals. And when I could pedal, I couldn't get traction and my tires would spin.

Once, I was riding along and a horse joined me on the road for a run. There was no fence anywhere and I don't know where he came from or where he was going. He was chestnut brown with a star on his forehead and seemed to enjoy having a running partner. He kept pace with me for about ¼ mile and then he trotted off the road and into the woods. Go figure.

At the Yukon border the road intersected with the Alaska Highway (also called the Alcan), and we turned right towards Watson Lake. There was a long stretch of good pavement for about five to six miles toward the Liard River Crossing. A motorcycle pulled up alongside me and the riders, a couple from Illinois, and I carried on a very amiable conversation as we rode. They had ridden to Anchorage and were now heading home. They would be home before I would get to Alaska.

The road was the first sustained paved road we'd been on for a while and it was easy compared to the roads we had just left. I was just cranking it out when the man asked me how fast I thought I was going. I told him I didn't have a clue and he said twenty-nine miles an hour. Considering I was pedaling a fully loaded touring bike weighing about eighty-five pounds, on flat ground, I was pretty pleased!

The motorcyclist said "Good luck" and pulled away. I was having a great time. The road was great, the weather was ideal and I was happy. After the Laird River Crossing, the road turned uphill for three to four miles then dropped downhill for the last few miles into Watson Lake.

16

July 13–15

✦

1,970 miles from Missoula

Watson Lake was home to an amazing assortment
of signs from all over the world.

As we rode into Watson Lake after seventy-four miles, we came upon the famous Watson Lake Signposts. A homesick G.I., Carl K. Lindley, from Danville, Illinois, helping to build the Alaska Highway in 1942, put up a sign from his hometown. Soon, there were signs from other G.I. hometowns, and the tradition still continues. There must have been several thousand signs, from towns such as Worms, West Germany; Ida Grove, Iowa; Troy, Michigan. There were even a few with Japanese characters. Someone from Portsmouth, Virginia, was busily nailing a sign to a small open spot next to a sign from Winder, Georgia.

Our home for the night was a provincial campground with a shelter that we commandeered for our kitchen. We ate our fill of omelets, fruit, yogurt, and salad. Our appetites were trying to keep up with our calories. It was a Bacchanalian feast, and we couldn't gorge ourselves enough! We were eating so much we could have fueled a small village.

The campgrounds in Canada hosted all sorts of travelers, from tent campers like us, all the way up to really fancy RV's. Campgrounds, by their very nature, require folks to coexist in a small space, and encourage an *"in tune"* sense of community. Most of the time, people recognized that there were others around, and kept their noises to a minimum. Occasionally, someone would come into a campground in their own self-absorbed world with no idea that others were around them. Not long after dinner on our first night in Watson Lake, an RV came in and immediately parked next to our collection of tents, even though there were plenty of vacant spots, farther back into the campground. When the dust settled, the driver got out and cranked up his generator which sounded like a badly tuned lawn mower, only louder. We assumed he would turn it off as soon as his dinner was finished and we sat in the picnic shelter struggling to carry on a conversation over the noise. As it got dark, it became apparent to us that the RV occupant was planning on running the generator all night, which I suppose was for his electric toothbrush, TV, and air conditioning. The occupant of the RV was amazingly oblivious to the noise and the aggravation he was causing the other campers in Watson Lake. Pretty soon, our picnic shelter became the headquarters of other disgruntled campers who had come to share their feelings of frustration at the RV owner. Democratically, it was decided someone should go and nicely ask them to turn off the generator because it was disturbing everyone in the vicinity. Undemocratically, I was volunteered for the job. I knocked on the door and the man opened it to see me and about twenty others in the background.

"Whatta'dya want?" He'd had a few beers and appeared to be running on fumes.

"We'd like to ask if you wouldn't mind shutting your generator down for the night?"

"Why would I wanna do that?"

"Well, it would be a lot quieter, and all these people (I pointed to the group) will be able to get a little sleep."

He motioned for me to lean toward him.

"You can tell them to #@%&* off! I paid for my spot, and I can run my generator if I want to."

And he slammed the door in my face.

I expect no one in the campground slept very much that night. To make matters worse, he was outside at 5 AM, noisily banging things together. He pulled out shortly afterwards and headed south. Embarrassingly, he was American.

Our breakfast the next morning consisted of skillet-sized pancakes with bananas or blueberries in the batter. I had six.

Now was the time for bike maintenance, and I had to find a place to weld my rear rack back together after it had come apart on the rough roads of British Columbia. I rode around until I found a shop where a man welded it back together for $10. We had sent another set of tires and tubes apiece to Watson Lake so we wouldn't have to carry them. Most of the group had to put on at least one new tire because the gravel roads were very hard on the sides of the tires. I had already done that at Boya Lake, so all I needed to fix now was one of my pedals. A ball bearing had broken inside of it and that was causing the pedal to stick.

We found a Laundromat with showers and spent several hours trying to wash the grime of the dirt roads from ourselves and our clothes.

Watson Lake is generally considered the first stop in Yukon for travelers heading north up the Alaska Highway. It was first settled by American Frank Watson and his father in 1897 after they had finished working their claim in the Klondike Gold Rush.

It became an important hub for soldiers building the Alaska Highway during 1942. The American army, fearing an invasion of Alaska by the Japanese, built the over 1,500-mile road from Dawson Creek, BC to Fairbanks, Alaska, in a little over eight months. Watson Lake remains an important distribution center for mining, logging, and communications.

We got a late start for the fifty-two mile ride to Simpson Lake the next day because we had to make a grocery-store run since there would be no stores for a couple of days. All of us pitched in to carry something and I tied five loaves of bread from my bike. It looked as if

A lonely stretch on the Robert Campbell Highway in Yukon.

there were icicles hanging from a Christmas tree.

We headed north on the Robert Campbell Highway, into the wilds of Yukon and our next rest day in Carmacks.

Almost immediately, we hit gravel and the road became almost unrideable. There were big chunks of stone embedded in hard dirt that rattled the whole bike. After a few miles, we ran into a road repair crew that had just dumped some sort of gooey liquid on the road, and it was messy. The road was almost like quicksand for several miles. Our tires sank into it, and we got mired down. Worse, the glop stuck to our tires and clogged our fenders so much that we had to stop every hundred yards and clean them out with a stick so our wheels would roll. It was hard riding, too, because it was like riding in our highest gears even though we were on a flat road. It probably took us an hour to ride through the three or four miles of road goo and it expended a lot of energy needed on our ride.

John eating an onion sandwich
beside the road.

As I was riding into the campground at Simpson Lake, my front tire went flat and I had to push the bike the last 200 yards. The sharp rocks of the day had cut my tire and gone into my tube. It was my first flat of the trip. I pushed my bike to the picnic shelter and started the task of changing my tire with my expensive little tire irons I had purchased before the trip. My front tire had a big cut place on it that couldn't be fixed, so I had to pitch it, change the rear tire back to the front, and put one of the new tires that I had shipped to myself on the back.

Simpson Lake is a very long lake that is curiously shallow. The water is crystal clear and Dale waded to a spot that must have been at least 150 yards from shore and he was only in waist-deep water. It's a good thing Dale didn't have any swimming problems while he was way out in the lake because none of us could have gotten to him quickly, he was so far out.

Dale was an interesting guy, although I never felt that I got to know him very well. He had most recently taught cross-country skiing for the Von Trapp family, at their lodge in Stowe, Vermont. Previously, he had worked as an engineer, and was very analytical and unemotional as I remembered his quick-to-the-point-without-niceties comments during my knee problems. He had gone through a nasty divorce, and had decided to chuck it all for the life of a "gentleman vaga-bond" for a few years. He had done extensive camping, and had led a Trans-American tour a few years earlier. Dale had apparently made some good money as an engineer because his clothing and equipment were all top of the line. He looked as if he were a biking catalogue model, whereas the rest of us looked like we had purchased our mismatched clothes and equipment at a yard sale. He was about thirty-seven, but looked to be in the best visible shape of all of us. His arms, legs, and abdominal muscles were all well defined and he looked as if he could play wide receiver in the NFL. Most days, if the sun was out, he would go shirtless to work on his tan, and as a result, he was bronze, while the rest of us were embarrassingly pale when we went shirtless. He could be funny, and had a raucous laugh, but could be prickly and short, probably without realizing it. Or, maybe he *did* realize it. I don't know. Dale seemed to always hold something back emotionally from the group, which might have been a consequence of his divorce. Consequently, I don't think anyone else got to know him very well either. He did talk a few times about entering dental school after the trip, and I remember thinking he'd probably make a good dentist if he worked on his "bed-side manner."

John decided he wanted to keep his onion and cheese sandwich cool during the night. He found a tin container like the one where your grandmother might keep her cookies. Then, he put the tin containing the sandwich into the water at the edge of our campsite and tied it with a small rope. About an hour later, Arnold looked up and said, "John, isn't that your food floating down the lake?" Sure enough, John's sandwich tin had floated off and was about 100 yards off-shore. John let out a few choice words as he ran around the campground asking the other campers if they had a rowboat that he could borrow to retrieve his lunch. He drew an appreciative crowd on the shore when he was finally able to procure a boat and paddle out to his lunch, and then good-naturedly took a good ribbing when he got back.

Francis Lake was our destination after a fifty-eight mile ride from Simpson Lake. Francis Lake is the second largest lake in the Yukon, and Tim and I were so exhausted from the ride that we collapsed on the shore and took a nap. The day started out bright and clear, and the riding wasn't that hard; it was just hot, and the heat really took it out of us.

Garry and I rode together in the morning. We had stopped at a small store called Wilma and Ben's for a muffin when were surprised to see a porcupine saunter across the road and head towards us. It had to weigh forty to fifty pounds and was just bristling with quills that neither Garry, nor I, wanted sticking from our bodies.

The porcupine had a full head of steam and seemed intent on visiting with us. We quickly moved away from the store and hopped onto our bikes, much like cowboys in B movies, and headed for the road. The porcupine followed for a ways then turned back, satisfied that he had kept the area clear of bikers.

Garry liked to work at temporary jobs during the winter so he could lead bike trips in the summer. He was from Wisconsin originally, and had spent a harrowing year in Vietnam in the early 70's, while stationed in the Mekong Delta in the signal corps. I tried to get him to talk about his time there, but he wouldn't say much of substance. I *could* see a kind of faraway look in his eyes that indicated he'd seen more than he wanted to share. He had been a teacher at one point, but had most recently worked in a sporting goods store in Anchorage after he had led the trip the year before. Garry probably had the driest, wryest sense of humor of the group. In fact, I found him to be the funniest guy on the trip, in a warped sort of way, although his quips were almost lost because he talked so quietly. He wore a black wool hat most of the time (his hair appeared to be thinning), and had a certain fondness for really tough rides. Garry would wax eloquent about the romance of gravel roads and hard-to-ride hills. You could see that he really got pumped up at a riding challenge, and his morning discussions about the days upcoming ride always got me fired up, too. He was probably the best overall athlete on the trip. He was a strong rider, but he could throw a baseball or Frisbee with equal skill. Garry was very organized. He kept meticulous records on distances and locations as well as the group finances. He watched the group expenses so well, that we all received a refund of about $150 at the end of the trip. I think he was toying with the idea of starting his own bike touring company, and wanted to use this trip as a dress rehearsal. I know he mentioned wanting to organize a biking tour of China sometime within the next year after our ride. Garry could be a bit of a loner, but was very focused on making sure the trip was a success. I'm sure he felt a great deal of disappointment (we all did) when Pete, Tom, and Steve left the trip, thinking that if he had done something, noticed something, or said something differently, they may not have quit. I will always be grateful for the quiet encouragement he gave me during my knee problems, and for the times he graciously rode at a snails pace to keep me company.

The Robert Campbell Highway wasn't much wider than a lane of an interstate and wasn't heavily traveled. Arnold counted thirty-three vehicles that passed him all day on the ride to Francis Lake. The Campbell Highway is considered a main road, though, and we had to be careful to watch for vehicles coming up from behind and not slowing as they passed.

The ride the next day would be a really tough one, according to Garry. He said it would be about sixty miles with lots of hills and the likelihood for more bad gravel. He specifically noted that there were two hills that were so steep that he had had to push his bike up and over them the year before. One of those hills was extremely steep with bad gravel, and that made it memorable. To that hill he gave the name "True Grizz."

I went to bed early in order to get a good start before the heat.

17

July 16–17

✦

2,094 miles from Missoula

The ride to Big Campbell River was everything Garry said it would be. Although we didn't have any more goo to deal with, the gravel was really bad, and there were many hills that required some serious concentration. I was riding alone because I was so psyched about getting over True Grizz Hill that I was impatient to leave the campsite.

The day was hot and clear and I had just about used all the water in my water bottles by the time I got to True Grizz Hill. The road turned, then straightened and leveled out for a mile. And suddenly, there it was at the end of the mile long straightaway, looming ahead and looking like an earthen dam. It was awesome and intimidating at the same time. It was probably 1/3 of a mile in length. There were no turns; it just went straight over the hill. The gravel was so bad it was visible from a mile away. It was time to see who was boss!

I got a good running start and kept going. A few times my rear wheel lost traction but I was able to keep my balance and in no time I was at the top. It was way too easy. There had been several hills in B.C. that seemed to me to be much harder. In fact, I was barely breathing hard.

I was, however, out of water. So I waited, and waited, and waited for the others to show up. After forty-five minutes, I was very thirsty and I flagged down the first vehicle I had seen in about two hours, an RV that had just chugged up the same hill. It pulled off to the side of the road and the driver, Jay, and his wife, Pat, climbed down and introduced themselves.

"Do you have a flat tire?" said Pat.

"No, but I sure could use some water if you have any extra to spare."

Jay said, "We have plenty. Say, are you with some other bikers?"

"I am. Did you see them?"

"We saw them all swimming in Finlayson Creek a few miles back. Looked like they were skinny dipping"

"That figures," I said.

Then Pat said, "It's noon, and we were going to stop anyway. How would you like to have lunch with us? We have tuna sandwiches and ice cold Pepsi in the cooler."

"I would be delighted," I said. My initial shyness at being offered food from strangers had long since disappeared.

We climbed up into the RV, which was air conditioned, and Pat expertly laid out a feast of tuna sandwiches, chips, fruit, cookies, Fig Newtons, and cold Pepsi. Jay and Pat, from Texas, were newly retired and decided an extended RV trip would be a great way to begin the next stage of their life together. They left Texas and were heading to Alaska. Then, they would backtrack and head east through Canada, see the eastern U.S. states, and then head down to winter in the Florida Keys. They expected to travel for about a year before heading home.

I was happy to benefit from the fortunate convergence of my trip and their trip. It sure was nice to sit in a cool RV and have something besides peanut butter and jelly for lunch.

Eventually, the others showed up after their swim. Jay and Pat offered everyone some cookies and Pepsi. We even had a little impromptu birthday celebration for Garry when we put a match into a Fig Newton and lighted it like a birthday candle.

After a while, we all needed to be on our way. Jay filled all our water bottles and bade us farewell and a good ride. They disappeared northward in a cloud of dust.

The Yukon is an interesting place. It is described as a semi-arid desert. It was amazingly dry, and the trees, which were evergreen, were short and stubby. It is also really, really quiet. It is the profound type of quiet that lies upon you…Almost like the quiet when there is a really big snowfall. Robert Service, in his famous poem "The Spell of the Yukon," said:

It's the great, big, broad land 'way up yonder,
It's the forests where silence has lease;
It's the beauty that fills me with wonder,
And the stillness that fills me with peace.

There was virtually no traffic. There were none of the everyday sounds to which we are accustomed: No airplanes, no jack hammers, no cars or trucks. Just quiet.

Now we have a new insect aggravation to add to mosquitoes and black flies. Deerflies! They started appearing about the time we left True Grizz Hill and plagued us for several days as we rode through the Yukon wilderness. The deerflies appeared to be much like a horsefly, except more determined and meaner.

My first encounter with the deerfly was when I was taking a lunch break on the side of the road and felt a sharp bite on my shoulder blade. I reflexively jumped with surprise as I saw the deerfly flying just out of range.

The bite drew blood, and the deerfly kept buzzing around me looking for an opening to bite again. I swatted at him, which only seemed to tick him off, and started pedaling up the road to lose him. This didn't damper his enthusiasm at all, and only made him more interested. He was unbelievably arrogant for an insect. Imagine a bug with a chip on his shoulder flying alongside of me for what must have been several miles, just out of reach of my furiously swatting hand. "Ha, you inferior human! See me fly within reach and dart away with impunity!"

It was a strange scene: a biker pedaling and muttering furiously on a gravel road, while flailing at a cocky deerfly. On and on we traveled together in a high speed chase. Finally, he got a little too close, and I nicked him enough to make him spin off into the weeds next to the road.

The day was a long, hard sixty mile ride to Big Campbell River. It was hot, there was bad gravel, it was against the wind, and I had had to race a deerfly. We camped next to a small Indian village next to the river. There were several tiny log cabins that seemed to hold 10 or more people in each. There were rusted cars and dismantled snowmobiles everywhere, and you could tell that life was hard for these folks. They treated us with kindness and we gave them some fish that John had caught in the river as payment for letting us camp on their land.

Another tough day awaited us on the sixty-four mile ride from Big Campbell River to the Lapie Campground, several miles past Ross River. It was another hard slog against the wind with terrible gravel. The land was really dry, and we rode through an area that had just had a forest fire. I watched with interest as a helicopter flew back and forth between the fire and a lake where it would fill up a large bucket of water suspended underneath, and dump it directly on the fire.

Our new nemesis, the deerfly, was out again-with reinforcements! They would come out of nowhere if I stopped for more that a moment, then they would follow in a kind of formation one might see bombers flying in old World War II movies. Occasionally, the sun would be at my back and I could see my shadow ahead of me. And there, keeping pace would be several deerflies that would show up as tiny shadow dots next to my own shadow. Sometimes, they would crisscross at high speed a couple of feet in front of my nose like the Navy fighter exhibition team, the Blue Angels. It was really annoying and I tried to smack them as they flew by. It was not very successful, and sooner or later they grew tired of the chase and I would be alone again, until the next stop brought more out in force.

Garry had mentioned there were two turnoffs to get to Ross River, which was a few miles off the road. He said the first turnoff would save about ten miles of riding and seemed to me to be the obvious choice. He also said it was steeper. Now that was an understatement!

I got to the turnoff at about 1:30 PM and started up. The hill was incredibly steep. It made True Grizz Hill look like an anthill. The road was curvy and kept winding upward for three miles. I had to walk most of the way because I couldn't get traction and because it felt as if I was going to topple over backwards.

The greatest swimming hole in history at the Lapie Campground outside of Ross River, Yukon.

"Hey buddy!" said guy in a pick-up truck as he pulled up next to me and offered me a lift down the other side which, amazingly, was steeper. I happily took him up on it and we skidded down the other side and into the settlement of Ross River. Again, I was there before everyone else, and I spent my time drinking copious amounts of apple juice, Coca-Cola, and water to quench my thirst. I had again used up my water in the heat and dust on the Campbell Highway. Ross River was a dusty little grouping of a few buildings: a grocery store, hotel, town hall, but oddly, not many houses. From town, I could see for miles off to the north. There, in the distance, was the great and deep Yukon. It was beautiful and a little disconcerting to look at so much nothingness. Ross River, except for a radio playing melancholy Canadian pop music, was really quiet.

I had ridden hard for the past couple of days to beat the heat, and now it was catching up to me. I was worn out and we had another eight or so miles to go before we got to the Lapie Campground. I found a shaded corner, sat down, had a sandwich, and promptly went to sleep. Tim woke me up after about thirty minutes just as the others were pulling into town.

We loaded up with groceries and headed out of town by the second route, which was hilly but not as jaw-droppingly steep.

Our campsite at Lapie River was one of the most gorgeous of the trip. Garry remembered that there was a campsite down a trail from the main camping area. We walked our bikes down the trail which opened up inside a small canyon cut through by the river. We pitched our tents in a flat area in a grove of trees about fifty feet from the water. Also located about fifty feet away was what had to be "History's Best Swimming Hole." Eons of water cutting through the rock had formed a natural bowl that was about four feet deep and thirty feet across. There was enough water running through it to make a refreshing, but not dangerous, whirlpool.

Naturally, we all needed a bath and wandered down for a skinny dip. We were fairly close to the highway bridge crossing the river but, at this stage of our trip, we were almost beyond normal modesty. The water was frigid, too. I suppose we were all so acclimated to our surroundings and cold that we were able to stay in for a long time just leisurely swimming and bathing. The same water temperature in Montana caused me to almost come out of my skin, and now I found it invigorating. I could tell my grandkids "Yep, I was a bad dude. I swam in water full of ice cubes, and it didn't bother me at all." I was becoming Grizzly Adams.

On the ride to Ross River and to our campsite, we counted seventeen vehicles all day during a sixty-four mile ride. I was passed by one truck that gave me the worst dusting to date on the whole trip. He zoomed by me pulling along a dust cloud that engulfed everything around it like a tornado. There was dirt, dust, rocks and heat from the truck spraying all around. The day was hot and I was sweaty, and I had the odd experience of having the dust on my arms, legs, and face, turn to mud.

18

July 18–20

✦

2,251 miles from Missoula

I was really excited to be in the Yukon. I had read *Call of the Wild* as well as several poems by Robert Service that told stories about the Yukon. I thought of it as a kind of mystical place that you hear about but most people couldn't find on a map, even though it is one-third the size of the lower forty-eight states.

Alexander Mackenzie traveled the area in 1789 and floated northward down the Mackenzie River (which he had graciously named after himself), to the Arctic Ocean, where he learned about another great river, the Yukon, across the mountains to the southwest.

Over time, fur traders (Russian, Canadian, British, and American) began setting up outposts in the wilderness and along Yukon's rivers. In 1867, Russia sold Alaska to the United States, and independent American traders began using steamboats to cruise up the Yukon River from Alaska and into the interior of the Yukon.

During the 1870's, gold prospectors looking for new areas to mine filtered into the Yukon from British Columbia and worked the rivers and creeks until the big gold strike at Bonanza Creek, outside of Dawson City, in 1896.

Three itinerant gold miners-George Carmack, Skookum Jim, and Dawson Charlie-hit paydirt on Bonanza Creek, a tributary running into the Klondike River. It wasn't long before word got out, and miners and wannabe miners flooded the area looking to get rich. There were rumors that gold nuggets the size of cannonballs could be picked straight out of the rivers.

Within months, word of the gold find had traveled to America and southern Canada, and thousands flocked to the Yukon. Dawson City was the epicenter of the rush. Located where the Klondike and Yukon Rivers converged, Dawson boomed to over 40,000 people, making it the largest city west of Winnepeg.

More than $95 million dollars of gold was mined from the region between 1896 and1903, but the boom was short-lived. When the mining went bust, many picked up stakes and moved to the next booming area: Nome Alaska.

The population of Yukon fell to below 5,000 by 1921, and remained low until the beginning of World War II, when over 30,000 American soldiers built the Alaska Highway through the Yukon Territory to transport military supplies to Alaska.

Mostly, the Yukon is miles and miles of wilderness crisscrossed by clear streams and rivers, and a few roads. The settlements are still like outposts: jumping off spots for excursions into the wild. It takes a hardy soul to live here; winters of unbearable cold and twenty-hour nights, summers of heat and bugs. Yukon is like water that seeps into nooks and crevices; it fills you and wraps itself around you. It engulfs you. It uses you, but you keep wanting more.

Our ride the next day was supposed to be a leisurely forty-four miles to Faro, but we decided to increase the mileage in the next two days in order to get to Carmacks a day early. We ended up riding sixty-six miles the first day and will ride seventy-four miles the second one out of Ross River.

I saw our RV buddies, Pat and Jay, again and met their friends Betty and Earl from Memphis. Pat and Jay invited me to have lunch with them at Little Salmon Lodge. I polished off my four sandwiches and was politely waiting for them to finish when Pat offered me her leftover lunch, which happened to be moose liver, onions and potato. I have never been excited about any sort of liver. It's the sort of stuff that looks really good until you take a big bite and the aftertaste just jumps up the back of your throat and into your nose. Then, it stays with you like the smell of a skunk.

Naturally, I said yes, I'd like some. Well, to my huge surprise, it tasted great with no aftertaste. I finished off what was left of the plate and could have gone another round. Jay and Pat had seen me eat in their RV a few days earlier, so they were used to seeing quantities of food disappear from my plate. Betty and Earl were unprepared and sat with a sort of awestruck look as I kept eating.

Finally, Earl said: "Jay, you told me about this young man and his eating. But I never would have believed it unless I had seen it with my own eyes."

I said that it was fun to eat like this now, but that I would need to slow down after the end of the ride; otherwise I would grow like a balloon.

We set up camp at the end of the day at a little rest area next to Drury Creek. We were all pretty tired. We had ridden about 300 miles in five days over some of the roughest roads and steepest hills we had experienced the whole trip. In addition, it was hot and buggy. We were looking forward to our rest day in Carmacks.

After our seventy-four mile ride the next day to Carmacks I wrote in my journal, "Go away, I'm too tired to write."

It took twenty-four hours for the physical and mental numbness of the last week's ride to wear off, particularly the last day into Carmacks from Drury Creek. That day started off hot, and Garry and I rode slowly together to conserve energy. We stopped several times for about thirty minutes each, and once we were standing next to the road when Dale rode by wearing nothing at all. There was no traffic, and he decided it would be funny to see how far he could ride with no clothes on. Later, he said he rode for several miles and was passed by a tour bus. He just waved and kept riding.

The Yukon River came into sight for the first time today and was majestic. From the road, it looked strong, fast, and deep, and appeared to be flowing from some formidable mountains from the south.

The route was, again, loaded with hills. There were three that stood out as "quality" hills, and we named them by degree of difficulty: Baby Bear, Mama Bear, and Papa Bear. All were steep. Baby Bear and Mama Bear were fairly short, maybe a mile each in length, but Papa Bear was long, maybe three curving miles, and had a road grade in places of about seven to ten %. Baby Bear and Mama Bear were strenuous. Papa Bear was more difficult.

By the time we started climbing Papa Bear I was at about my last thread of endurance. I had tried to ration my water but now it was gone. Garry and I just put our heads down and rode. It was a grind to get to the top. My legs were burning, I was sweating in big rivulets, my hands and shoulders ached from gripping the handlebars, and my knees were getting tender. The fatigue of riding so many miles had caught up with me. In a ride like that, I just kind of drifted off into a trance. Not conscious, not unconscious, just there. I was at my most basic: one with the road. Breathe, pedal, breathe, pedal. Up and up. It is a shared agony with the others that can be laughed about later. Just keep riding. Don't waste energy looking for the top, just keep going. Sweat was dripping from my nose as if I was sitting in a sauna. Sweat soaked through my shirt and blue jeans, which I rarely took off now.

Suddenly, we were at the top with a wonderful view of the valley ahead holding the small town of Carmacks. Dark clouds were rolling in. It was smooth sailing the last few downhill miles into town, and Garry and I pulled up in front of the little grocery store.

I spent the next half hour or so gulping cans of 7-Up, Ginger Ale, Root Beer, apple juice, and two pints of water. It was a great feeling of accomplishment every time we came into a town for a rest day. It was as if we riders were conquerors and we were able to triumphantly ride into town as heroes. Of course, the towns-people saw us only as smelly, scraggly bikers. This rest day in Carmacks was well earned: 374 miles in six days over hot, dusty roads and across the most consistently bad gravel of the whole trip.

Naturally, it started raining about the time everyone arrived at the store. Garry worked his magic again, and we moved into the sanctuary of a small church called the Gospel Chapel. Somehow he had made friends with the young minister and his wife while I was swigging soft drinks and water. They even offered up their shower at their home, which was a trailer through the woods behind the church. We had been roundly dusted the last couple of days and were very appreciative of the opportunity to knock some dirt off.

We slept late the next morning and had a large breakfast of cream of wheat, fruit, and granola. Then, since it was raining, we spent the whole day doing nothing but napping and recuperating from our ride from Watson Lake.

All throughout our trip we had been a fairly harmonious group. When strangers from all different walks of life are put together into a tight group for three months, one could expect some friction to develop at some point. We were pretty lucky that most of the time everyone was laid back and could take about anything that came along. That changed briefly in Carmacks. A feud had been quietly simmering for a couple of days between Arnold and Henry, of all people. Arnold was smarting from a recent Dear John letter from his girlfriend, and he made some off-handed comment to Henry about being old and slow. Henry took offense, but stayed quiet about it for several days. The pressure kept building along with our fatigue on the ride from Watson Lake, until Henry finally blew his top in Carmacks. We were eating our dinner outside of the chapel when Arnold again said something about Henry being old and slow. This really set Henry off. Henry launched into Arnold with a blistering torrent of words that caught all of us by surprise; most of all by Arnold who didn't know he had offended Henry. Henry vented some very choice words and phrases for a few minutes about being hurt by Arnold's comments until he ran out of steam, and stomped off to regain his composure. Arnold, taken aback, watched him with saucer eyes. The rest of us could see it coming, but were still surprised at mild-mannered Henry's creative uses of the English language. Arnold apologized profusely for his comments when Henry returned, and they shook hands and became better friends afterwards. In fact, they spent several weeks after the trip riding to the ferry that goes from Haines, Alaska, to Seattle, and then riding down the west coast.

19

July 21–25

✦

2,475 miles from Missoula

The next day, we were scheduled to ride forty-five miles to the town of Minto, and ride eighty-one miles the next day to Moose Creek. Mindful of how tired we had become on our ride from Watson Lake, and knowing that our next rest stop was 224 miles away, in Dawson City, we made a group decision to cut the 126 miles of the next two days into two rides in the sixties. We would stop at Pelly Crossing after the first day, and bypass Minto.

The results of a day of muddy riding on gravel roads in Yukon.

Arnold and I rode the sixty-one miles together all day. He was still mystified at the little tiff with Henry and kept saying that he didn't mean to hurt Henry's feelings. Arnold had graduated from the Colorado School of Mines and had ridden his bike from Colorado, through, Wyoming, and into Montana, where he had been living in Helena. He rode to Missoula to join our group. He had recovered from a kidney transplant, and took a boatload of medicine every day that he kept in a Tupperware container. I was surprised that his medicine had stayed intact during the rough roads. I had a plastic bottle of vitamins that were almost shaken to dust. Arnold's kidney issues didn't seem to affect his riding at all, and as far as I know he didn't suffer any after effects on the trip.

Arnold was riding on a racing bike that really wasn't appropriate for the rigors of long distance bike touring. Bike racers typically want bikes that are very responsive, and the wheelbase on racing bikes are usually shorter to enhance the responsiveness. Bike tourists generally want comfort and stability over long distances, and their bikes usually have a longer wheelbase. Think of the difference between a sports car and a van, and you get a pretty good idea why a touring bike would be a better choice on rough roads. Amazingly, he actually had fairly good success with it if one didn't count the 10 or 11 flat tires he'd had. He was really bothered about receiving the Dear John letter from his girlfriend back in Helena. They had agreed before the trip that she would join the trip in Watson Lake, and would finish the ride with us. She had indicated nothing different in all her letters during the early part of the trip. He had been so excited that for weeks he had been waking up every morning and singing cheesy wake up songs, which became annoying. When she backed out on him, it was absolutely unexpected, and he went into a funk for several days, which led to the argument with Henry. It had taken him several more days to get over being humiliated, and he had decided to move on to greener pastures after the trip.

We were rained on in the morning. The road was muddy and washboardy, but it was an easy ride compared to some of the more recent days.

We stopped for lunch on the side of the road and had the unusual experience of watching a small rain shower, not much wider than a hundred yards, come down the road toward us. When it got close, we ran into the trees next to the road and watched it pass without getting wet.

At Pelly Crossing, we met some guys who were riding what they called mountain bikes. We had heard about them, but it was our first opportunity to see some in action. They were clunky looking with big knobby tires, strong looking frames, and gears on the handlebar. The rider sits more upright than on a touring bike. One of the guys let me ride his bike around the parking lot, and I was pleasantly surprised to learn that it was easier to ride than my bike and a whole lot more comfortable. They said they hadn't had any flat tires, which made us envious-John and Arnold especially.

The next day, the sixty-five mile ride to Moose Creek was long and dull. There wasn't much scenery to speak of enroute other than a nice view atop a plateau that afforded a view of three sides of the Yukon wilderness.

As I reached Stewart Crossing, I met a biker who had ridden from Alaska on the Top of The World Highway, which we would be riding on after we left Dawson City. He said that the gravel was "terrible" and that it was "real hard riding." It was supposed to be a neat road to ride, so I looked forward to it anyway.

Garry and I bought groceries at the under stocked little store and made grilled cheese sandwiches because the vegetables and fruit were all mushed, withered, and pitiful looking.

John and Tim washing mud off Tim's bike at the Klondike Campground outside Dawson City.

It was a long eighty-five mile day, but it was actually kind of a fun ride the next day to Klondike Campground. Tim, John, and I rode together the whole day. John had a flat tire, which gave Tim and me an opportunity to make fun of him while he changed yet another tire. So far, I had had only one flat. Tim had had about three, and John was at about number twelve. We got a little wet during a brief shower; then the sun came out and the day was beautiful. We had enough energy to race the last eleven miles and didn't even mind getting slopped with mud. We stopped at Klondike Campground and immediately took our bikes and held them under the water pump to clean the mud off the bike chains and freewheels before it dried and had to be chipped off.

It was exciting to me to be in the land of the Klondike Gold Rush and I looked forward to learning all about it while we were in Dawson City, an ultra-easy thirteen miles away.

Fired up! What a great place to visit! We slept a little later than usual and had a long breakfast since we had to go only thirteen miles to Dawson. Tim and I rode together and turned off the main road toward the famous gold digs along Bonanza Creek. We rode past big piles of rocks, called "tailings," everywhere along both sides of the road. These piles were made by huge dredges that would dig up the earth, then filter it through a long revolving tube that functioned as a sifter. The sifter would tumble the dirt and rocks through small holes where they would be sifted again with the idea that gold nuggets, being larger than dirt, would end up as remainder. The stones too large to fit through the small holes would be sent by conveyor belt out the back of the dredge, where they would pile up. There is speculation that there are some huge gold nuggets too large to go through the small holes of the filter still under the tailing piles. But no one has yet come up with an economical method of finding those nuggets.

We rode back into history as we passed famous names of the gold rush like California Gulch, American Gulch, and Poverty Gulch, where miners worked long hours for "colors."

After several miles, we came across the remains of the largest gold dredge in North America, called Dredge #4. It was so big that the scoops of the dredge were the same size as a sofa love seat. There must have been fifty of these scoops. The chain holding the dredge boom hanging in the front was massive. Each link was as tall as a person. Tim stood next to one link and was dwarfed.

Diamond Tooth Gertie's Gambling Hall in Dawson City, Yukon. Home of the famous "Sour-Toe Cocktail."

Instead of our having to ride our bikes eight to nine miles back to the main road, a miner from California picked us up. We didn't get his name, but he came to Dawson in the summers and mined gold by hand, usually getting a little over an ounce a day. He was hoping to rent a bulldozer for the next summer on the assumption that it would be more efficient. He took us the short distance to Dawson, which gave us longer to poke around. Tim, Henry, and I took in a tour at the Palace Grand Theatre, where we planned to see the "Gas Light Follies" the next night.

We then took a tour on the sternwheeler "Keno" that used to travel the Yukon River between Dawson and Whitehorse.

At 4: 00 PM we went to the poet Robert Service's cabin and listened as an actor recited some of his poems. We enjoyed this immensely. Both Robert Service and Jack London lived in Dawson for a period of time during the gold rush. Both found that the area and characters provided fertile material for their writing.

Our campground was across the Yukon River from town and required a ride back and forth on a ferry. In Dawson, the Yukon was running fast and deep. There was a power to the river that was especially noticeable on the ferry for it had to chug hard to keep on a straight course for the landing on the other side.

We set up camp and went back across the river in order to make a visit to Diamond Tooth Gertie's Gambling Hall. Diamond Tooth Gertie's opened during the gold rush and is so named because Gertie had a diamond in one of her teeth. It is infamous as the home of the "Sour Toe Cocktail." This disgusting drink features dipping an ice cube with a severed toe frozen inside of it, into the drink. The ice cube is then taken out and returned to the freezer. Apparently, they had been doing this for years without the ice cube thawing and the toe falling into some poor slob's drink. Gertie's is the only legalized gambling hall in Canada and was doing a big business on the night we were there. There were high rollers winning and losing money with equal flair. Most of the gamblers had that mixture of elation and torment on their faces. They could be one card from a big haul or loss. None of us joined the betting crowd. There appeared to be an equal numbers of locals and tourists at the tables.

There was a spirited floor show that was more enthusiastic than skillful. Indeed, one of the dancing girls slipped and fell down in mid-can-can and good naturedly jumped back into the dancing line.

Garry and Tim riding the ferry across the Yukon River.

After about an hour and a half, we had had enough excitement and headed back to the campground. It was well past 11:00 PM, but it was still broad daylight. People who go to the top of Midnight Dome just outside Dawson, on June 21, the summer solstice, are supposed to be able to see the sun for 24 hours straight. It was July 24, and it would still be daylight for about twenty hours, while the other four hours were a kind of twilight. For us, it didn't really matter that the sun didn't go down because after having ridden for sixty to eighty miles, we were pretty tired. It was strange, however, to leave the tent in the middle of the night to go to the bathroom and see that it was still daylight.

The next morning, we took the ferry back across the river to Dawson for laundry and showers. While we were waiting for the laundry to finish, we did a little sightseeing through the gravel streets and were amazed to see abandoned buildings leaning at odd angles. We asked a local why the buildings were like that and he said that the ground in Dawson was permanently frozen several feet below ground. The phenomenon was called permafrost, and builders had to take it into account when erecting buildings; otherwise, the heat of the building would thaw the ground underneath, causing the building to lean at crazy angles. He pointed out one building that, he said, was the most photographed in all of Canada. It was photogenic in a wobbly sort of way.

Tim and I later visited the local museum that mainly had mining exhibits, and then we went to Jack London's cabin for a reading of some of his works. The cabin wasn't much more than one room with a small window. The roof was covered with sod for insulation. He reportedly wrote his well known book *Call of the Wild* while living there.

At dinnertime we heard that the town was going to have an all-you-can eat salmon bake. It was at the local park, and for $5 we were able to eat huge portions of salmon, baked potato, slaw, and bread. We went back for seconds and thirds, and it is likely they didn't make any money on us that night.

After dinner, our group took in the play *Gas Light Follies* at the Palace Grand Theatre. Somehow, we had the best seats in the house. We were close enough to see the actors sweating as they told the story of how Dawson was founded.

When the show was over, we headed back across the river with the idea of getting a good night's sleep prior to our much anticipated trek across the Top of the World Highway. It wasn't to be, however, because there was a rip roaring party going on at the campsite next to us. It was loud, the people were obnoxious, and it went on for much of the night even though we asked them to be quiet. None of us got much sleep and, frustrated, we got up at about 5:00 AM, ate breakfast, and left. I don't remember any of us being very quiet as we were taking our tents down or eating breakfast. It was probably lost on the partiers, though, because it wasn't likely that anything would wake them before the afternoon.

20

July 26–28

◆

2,663 miles from Missoula

The seventy-two mile ride on the Top of the World Highway to the settlement of Boundary, Alaska, was the most incredibly astonishing ride (even more so than Logan Pass) that most of us had ever attempted…and completed. The road was gravel, of course. It started off with a ten-mile hill immediately after leaving the campground. We didn't even have a chance to warm up before we started climbing. There were many, many more hills to follow-all going up. There didn't seem to be any downhills. The elevation of Dawson City was about 1000 feet and the highest point on the road was about 4,300 feet. We must have climbed a vertical mile when you factor in the few downhills that seemed few and far between.

The scenery was magnificent for around two hours with broad sweeping vistas of the Yukon wilderness, then the weather got nasty. It started to rain, and rain, and rain some more. The temperature dropped into the forties. We could see the rain squalls coming towards us up the valleys. We were above tree line, and there was no place to hide. So we just had to keep riding.

Tim and I were riding together when a coyote ran into the road just in front of us. It was small, maybe forty pounds. He was startled and took off up the road with Tim in hot pursuit and me trying to get a picture of them both. Tim followed him for about ¼ mile until the coyote leaped into the bushes next to the road and was gone.

The road crossed the top of treeless mountaintops and ridges. It was like a snake that wound off into the next set of clouds. There was nothing on either side of the road other than tundra and small bushes. Occasionally, the clouds would part and we would get a breathtaking view of miles and miles of mountains and tundra. When we got to the last hill leading to the Alaska border, the clouds had dropped, it was pouring rain, and we were surrounded by thick fog. The hill was about a mile in length and had a grade of 14% for most of it. On one side was a hill, on the other side, the road dropped off to nothingness. It might have been fifty feet or it might have been several hundred-we had no way of knowing. There was no guardrail. The hill was so steep that both Tim and I had to get off and push for the last 1/8 mile.

Tim and I reach the border of Alaska in a cold, foggy rain.

Even though the weather was the pits, I really enjoyed the ride. I have never felt so in tune with myself.

We stopped at the " Welcome to Alaska " sign, took pictures in the rain, then went to the border station to check in. We had been in Canada for over a month and a half.

The man that operated the border station lived with his wife in an apartment connected to the station. When he saw us come through the door dripping wet and chilled, he invited us into his apartment, where his wife kindly dried our rain jackets and made us hot chocolate. It was a great welcome back to the U.S. and rejuvenated us for the last few miles of riding to Boundary.

While we were inside the border station the weather miraculously cleared up. We rode mostly downhill into Boundary and waited for the others to arrive while we enjoyed a slice of pie in the cafe. Everyone made the ride without any problems except for Henry, who got tired and had to hitchhike the final few miles to Boundary.

Boundary, Alaska, is the official name of the settlement where we were spending the night. As far as I could tell, the settlement consisted of Action Jackson's Bar and the Boundary Café. Action Jackson's Bar sat next to a muddy parking lot. It was painted white with red trim and had a vinyl sofa sitting outside next to the front door. It had moose antlers over the door and a fifty-five gallon drum for burning trash next to it. Restrooms were a pit toilet around the corner of the building. The inside was dark and smoky and decorated in early Naugahyde, as well as the ubiquitous dollar bills stapled to the walls. I guessed that these dollar bills represented the retirement plan for the owner, assuming the bar didn't burn down first.

The Boundary Café was a small log cabin covered on the front with moose antlers, one of which was about five feet across. On one side of the building stood a propane tank that looked like a silver submarine. On the other side, we set up our camp amid old junked cars, fifty-five gallon drums, and a discarded table which we used as our cook table. We had a very restful night, even though we were camped near a bar in the wilds of Alaska.

The Top of the World Highway is where my real axle and freewheel broke apart spreading ball bearings all over the dirt road.

The road from Boundary to the settlement of Chicken was beautiful. There were broad green valleys, wild flowers, and vistas in all directions. The drawbacks were that there were tons of mosquitoes, and also that it sprinkled on us making forty-three of fifty-two days with some sort of precipitation.

About ten miles out of Boundary, my chain came off twice, which was easy enough to fix. A little later I was pedaling up a hill and suddenly I felt a jerk, then my pedals started spinning, and I looked back and saw that my freewheel looked as if it had exploded. The freewheel is the cluster of cogs that is located on the rear wheel, which along with the front chain ring, enable a biker to change gears. You pedal, shift gears, and the chain moves up or down the freewheel to make the riding easier.

I had never seen anything like it. Each cog of the freewheel was askew and I could see inside of it. This didn't look like a good sign. Tim and I had to wait with the mosquitoes until Garry caught up with his tool kit.

He looked at my freewheel and said, "Oh my gosh!"

I said, "What do you mean, 'Oh my gosh'?"

Garry said, "Well, this is not good."

Now I was really starting to get concerned.

"Your real axle has broken in two, and that caused your freewheel to break apart and spill about forty of the sixty ball bearings in the freewheel onto the dirt road."

"That sounds bad." I wasn't real sure what he was talking about, but I did understand his look of concern. I didn't even know bikes had axles.

He said, "We have an extra axle but I don't have enough ball bearings to replace all you lost. You need to find as many as you can in the dirt or else your freewheel won't work properly and you won't be able to change gears."

So I started crawling around on my hands and knees trying to find little silver ball bearings in the dirt. I was able to find a few, and Garry had about twenty ball bearings, so we were only able to replace about forty of the sixty ball bearings. Garry said that this arrangement would be temporary at best, and that there was a good chance that the freewheel could lock up on me at any time. But since we didn't have any other choice, we needed to go with it for now.

We started riding again and my bike seemed fine, although I noticed that the strut on my rear rack had broken again. Ten dollars wasted in Watson Lake! We pulled into Chicken, Alaska, at about lunch time and had our sandwiches outside of the Chicken Country Store. Chicken was named "Chicken" because the town leaders wanted to name the town Ptarmigan after the bird. No one, however, could spell Ptarmigan, so it is now Chicken. Chicken had a school, a store, a liquor store, and a bar. It was easy to see what the priorities of Chicken folk were. After lunch, we crossed over several rivers where people in wet suits were dredging for gold with small dredges on pontoons. We finally pulled into the campground on the Dennison River after a long, hilly day of fifty-six miles.

The next day, forty-nine miles into a ride of sixty-one miles, we would be ending our travels on gravel and get back to pavement permanently for the first time in about a month. We would intersect with the Alaska Highway and follow it to Fairbanks. Our mileage on gravel will have totalled about 1,300 miles.

The ride the next day was a real grind for the most part. We had a ten-mile uphill over Mt. Fairweather that was a nice ride. We could see the road snaking over the mountain from several miles out so we had an idea what was in store. The gravel over the mountain was exceptionally bad and made the riding tough. The view more than made up for the rough ride, though, and the downhill that followed was first class, although the gravel was tricky. I didn't want to crash and burn after all the time we'd spent on gravel, with just a few more miles till pavement. About six miles from Tetlin Junction (the intersection with the Alaska Highway) I came across some government fire fighters who offered me some cold Pepsi and some of their C-Rations. I had heard about C-Rations from former military guys, but I had never had any before. Well, the Pepsi was good, but the C-Rations left a lot to be desired. Nasty is the adjective that comes to mind.

Tim and I rode the last downhill to pavement and both almost crashed in the last hundred yards when we hit potholes covered with dust. The end of gravel came abruptly and without fanfare. It had been an amazing ride from Kitwanga Junction to Tetlin Junction. We had ridden the toughest roads and hills in North America. We had traveled past blue glaciers and forest fires, and through vast wilderness; carried our food for several days; experienced freezing temperatures and hot dry days; and seen bears, wolves, porcupines, and memorable towns. Now, we were back to some semblance of civilization and could expect heavy road traffic up the Alaska Highway to Fairbanks, our next rest stop three days away.

We turned north onto the Alaska Highway and headed for Tok twelve miles away. As soon as we turned onto pavement we rode into a stiff headwind. We were able to ride the twelve miles in a little under forty-five minutes, so I guess riding on the gravel had made us much stronger.

Riding on pavement again took some getting used to. On gravel, we needed to be alert for washboard roads, hidden potholes, and bad gravel. On pavement we didn't have to worry about road conditions as much as we had to concentrate on traffic. Both roads required a lot of concentration. It was just different.

After sixty-one miles, we pulled into a private campground in Tok that had showers-our first since Dawson City. Mighty Moe would be offended to know we didn't even have to build our own fire to heat the water. Arnold bought a big block of cheddar cheese and some Triscuits for an end-of-gravel celebration, and we quietly reflected on our mutual accomplishment. Someone said they felt sorry for Tom, Pete, and Steve because they missed such a cool ride. Strangely, I was feeling both jubilant and melancholy. Jubilant because of having ridden 1,300 miles on gravel road, and melancholy because I was having a great time and our trip would be ending in less than two weeks. Our group had become closer because of shared fun, misery, and exertions. In less than two weeks we would all be heading our separate ways and getting back to our normal lives. I didn't think any of us would ever be the same, though.

21

July 29–August 2

✦

2,927 miles from Missoula

AAARGH: the ride out of Tok was an extreme grind. We rode seventy-nine miles into a strong headwind, with few curves in the road, and not much in the way of scenery. Dale said, "Boy, the going is easy but it is hard to get started." Most of the rivers we crossed on the way to Big Gerstle River had a cloudy color called "Glacial Milk." The glaciers pulverize rock into dust which makes its way into the rivers. We didn't take into account that we couldn't drink the water and we had to resort to bumming water from RV's that we came across. Our group was beginning to burn out with exhaustion again, and we were looking forward to our rest day in Fairbanks so we could recuperate from the last few days of hard riding.

Our ride to Harding Lake was another long day in the saddle. We rode eighty-five miles, much of it into a headwind. After thirty miles, we stopped at Delta Junction to buy groceries and fill up our six gallon collapsible plastic jugs with water. There would be no more stores before Harding Lake and no place to get fresh water. Just so we wouldn't forget about our experience on gravel, we had to ride across eleven miles of some of the worst gravel of the whole trip with all of our groceries and water. I was carrying a jug of water that was full. So if a gallon of water weighs about six pounds, those of us with water aboard were carrying an extra thirty-six pounds on our bikes. After Delta Junction, we had to ride another 55 miles with this extra weight to Harding Lake.

Tim and I rode under the Alaska Pipeline, built to carry oil from the North Slopes of Alaska to the coast at Valdez, Alaska, where it would be shipped around the world. About 800 miles in length, the pipeline itself was a modern engineering feat. To reach Valdez, it had to cross 800 streams and rivers, and it cost over $8 billion dollars to build in 1977. The part we saw was crossing a river and the road with suspension cables holding it above the water like the Golden Gate Bridge.

The beer-swilling horse at the Richardson Roadhouse on the road to Fairbanks.

We stopped for lunch at a run-down bar called the Richardson Roadhouse. We were eating our sandwiches in the parking lot, and to our surprise, a horse walked out of the roadhouse door and walked towards us. The horse was full grown and started following us around trying to get at our sandwiches. We would move and he would follow. This went on for several minutes until he apparently grew bored with us and went back inside the roadhouse.

Of course, we had to follow him inside to see what was going on. Inside, the regular crowd was there, mainly afternoon drunks. The horse was standing in the middle of the floor slurping what looked like beer from a bucket. I jokingly asked someone if the horse had a drinking problem. He said, "No, looks like he's drinking just fine." The regulars weren't paying any attention to the horse. It was just a normal day at the Richardson Roadhouse.

Our stop for the night, Harding Lake, has some history behind it. President Warren G. Harding visited there at some point, but it was more famous as the lake from which Will Rogers and Wiley Post took off on their ill-fated plane trip to Pt.Barrow on the North Slope.

The forty-eight mile ride to Fairbanks was super easy, and after several long, grinding days, we were glad to have it. We did thirty miles from Harding Lake in two hours because the road was 99% flat. Dale, Tim, and I stopped in the town of North Pole, Alaska, just outside of Fairbanks. We visited the very campy Santa Claus House that was painted with Christmas scenes and sported the self-proclaimed "World's Largest Santa Claus" (made of wood) outside. Inside, it had Christmas ornaments, tee shirts, doo-dads, and other touristy stuff. We did learn that North Pole, Alaska, is one of the places to which letters addressed to Santa Claus are sent.

North Pole, Alaska. The home of letters to Santa Claus.

Feeling froggy, we rode the last eighteen miles into Fairbanks in a blistering forty-eight minutes. We arrived in Fairbanks just as th e rain did and finagl ed another indoor s tay at another churc h-owned house. There was a Baskin-Robbins Ice Cream shop near o ur house, and John and I went for milkshakes. I had a chocolate shake, then another chocolate shake, then a strawberry shake, all in about ten minutes. John had something similar, and we left the guy making milkshakes shaking his head in wonder. For dinner, we all walked to the local Pizza Hut and filled up on large quantities of salad and pizza.

Interestingly, we were all feeling very upbeat and had a spring in our step. We knew that the hardest part of the trip was behind us and that we had only seven days and about 300 miles to go. We could see the light at the end of the tunnel that had been hard to see while we were riding long miles through B.C. and Yukon. The long, grinding days on gravel were behind us.

We spent our rest day in Fairbanks mostly inside napping and doing laundry because it had started to rain and the temperature had dropped to about 45F. This day of rain made forty-seven days of precipitation, out of fifty-eight, with a week still to go.

Our sixty-eight mile ride from Fairbanks to the Shade Tree Campground was fairly normal. There were a few three and four-mile long hills, and the weather was bad. At the beginning of the trip, I was intimidated by long hills and struggled up them under great discomfort. Now, after so many miles, I went up the same types of hills without even flinching. Heck, sometimes I wasn't even breathing hard when we got to the top. We had been rained on plenty since my crazy fit on the road to Stewart. Rain now had no effect, either.

Our camping stop for the night was supposed to be the town of Nenana. We arrived there feeling good after fifty-three miles, and decided to ride another fifteen miles to the Shade Tree Campground. We did stop in Nenana long enough to go to a café for a milkshake and a piece of pie. Clearly, I thought, I was going to have a difficult time cutting down on these treats after the ride was over.

Nenana is famous as the home of the "Nenana Ice Classic" and also is the place where Warren G. Harding drove the golden spike signifying the end to construction on the Alaska Railroad. The Nenana Ice Classic is touted as "Alaska's Biggest Guessing Game." In the winter, a large tripod topped with a flag is erected on the ice of the Tanana River, which runs next to Nenana. Bettors can wager on the date and time at which the thawing ice will begin moving downstream in the spring, toppling the tripod. A full-time security guard is stationed next to the river to make sure no one cheats. This is no doubt part of Alaska's answer to Las Vegas.

22

August 3–5

◆

2,995 miles from Missoula

Mt. McKinley, Alaska.
I had reached my visual goal, but I needed a shower.

What a nice day we had on our ride from the Shade Tree Campground!

The weather had cleared, although it was still cool, and the fifty-three mile ride was mostly flat, except for a few hills to keep things interesting. We rounded a bend and off in the distance loomed Mt. McKinley. We were about 130 miles away, and it just dwarfed everything around it. Denali Park, which holds Mt. McKinley is larger than the state of Massachusetts. At 20,320 feet, Mt. McKinley is the highest mountain in North America, and is considered to be the world's largest exposed mountain. It is far higher than anything around it, unlike Mt. Everest, which is surrounded by so many other tall mountains that it is hard to appreciate how high it really is. There is no confusion about Mt. McKinley. Measuring from the base at 2,000 feet, to the summit at 20,320 feet, the 18,000 feet of exposed rock is more even than Mt. Everest. The Athabascan native people gave the mountain a very apt name: "High One."

Mt. McKinley is covered with glaciers and is so large that it makes its own weather. Temperatures at the top can dip as low as-95F, and winds as high as 150 miles per hour have been recorded. Climbers have always been fascinated with reaching the top of McKinley, and regularly take several weeks or more to reach the summit. I had been looking forward to our time in the park. We had heard that McKinley was hidden by clouds over 60% of the time. I had made seeing Mt. McKinley one of my goals, and I desperately wanted to see the mountain. It looked as if the weather gods were finally giving us a break.

As we got closer to the park entrance, the mountain moved from view. In Denali Park, the ecosystem is so fragile the park has all sorts of rules and regulations about traffic. There is only one road into and out of the park. Traffic is limited to park-owned buses that had to be used by anyone wanting to go to the interior of the park to see the scenery and in hopes of getting a glimpse of the mountain. The buses run on a reservation system whereby riders had to get free tickets as much as a day in advance. We planned to get our tickets when we arrived and take the earliest bus possible. We thought we would have more opportunities to see wildlife and have exploring time with an early time.

The Morino Campground was not far from the entrance of the park and was across the road from the hotel, store, and gas station. There was also an airstrip where Henry booked a sightseeing flight around the mountain for $70. I wasn't sure that the weather would hold the next day, so I gave him my camera to snap a few pictures of the mountain for me if we should miss it. We watched him take off towards the west. It was a gorgeous night. The clouds were few and fluffy, the sunlight angled in and gave everything a sharpness and crispness that almost snapped with clarity. The temperature was dropping; it was August 3, almost fall in this part of the world.

After a couple of hours or so, Henry came back and had a look of absolute wonder and awe in his eyes. He said the mountain was so beautiful that he had had a "near religious experience" as they flew around it and then to see some of the park. We were hoping the clear spell would continue through the next day.

Vast is a good word to describe Denali National Park. After a good sleep, we woke up at 4:45 AM to eat and be at our bus for the 6:00 AM departure. I knew it had been cold during the night, but when I climbed from my tent I was hit square in the face with a shocking blast of cold air. Our tents were covered with a heavy frost and our breath hung in the air. We made a quick breakfast and headed to the bus stop. There was a thermometer at the ticket booth and it registered 23F. That day, August 4, was the coldest of the whole trip. By now, we were used to being outside in any weather, so even though it was freezing we weren't in undue discomfort. The tourists around us, though, looked as if they were in pain. Most didn't look like they had taken into account that they would be in Alaska at the beginning of an Alaskan fall, and were wholly unprepared clothing-wise. Some were wearing tee-shirts and shorts. Some had flimsy looking jackets, and some looked like they were going to a Junior League picnic.

We climbed aboard a big yellow school bus and started off to our destination, Wonder Lake, eighty-five miles away, the area closest to the mountain that the bus would go. The standing rule on the bus was that if you saw any sort of wild-life, the bus driver would stop the bus for pictures out the windows. It was also a standing rule that passengers that wanted to hike could ask the driver to stop any-where along the route and they could get out. They could hike as long as they wanted as long as there were buses going by to pick them up. The implicit under-standing was that they would hike at their own risk.

It wasn't long before someone saw a moose and we stopped. A while later, we saw a herd of caribou, still later we saw a couple of grizzly bears off in the dis-tance. During the trip to Wonder Lake and back, we counted seven grizzly bears, eight moose, countless dall sheep and caribou, ptarmigan, marmots, marsh hawks, and who knows how many other animals.

Our bus crossed broad, treeless valleys (the treeline started at about 2,700 feet in elevation, so we were above it most of the day); valleys lush with birch, aspen, and willow trees; alpine meadows bursting with wild flowers; tundra; and wide, shallow rivers. The ground vegetation was as bright a green as anything I'd ever seen. We stopped for a viewpoint at Polychrome Pass and discovered a stunning view across the valley of different colored strata in the rock. Everywhere you looked, the scenery and wildlife was breathtaking. There were scrubby trees with moose lingering; huge fields of tundra with caribou, snowcapped mountains, and then, the mountain itself came into view. And boy, was it magnificent! We stopped at the Eielson Visitor Center, which offered a view of the mountain from about thirty miles away, and were almost struck dumb at the sight. It was almost mystical. I didn't want to take my eyes off of it for fear that it would disappear behind some unseen clouds. People talked in hushed tones out of a sense of awe and reverence.

We got aboard and kept going deeper into the park. Eventually, we got to Wonder Lake, about 15 miles from the base of the mountain. There was a camp-ground there that was used by normal folks, like us, and by climbers using it as a base camp for their assault on the mountain. The campground was exposed to the elements; there were no trees and not much vegetation other than scrubby bushes and tundra. It was really windy, and we saw two tents uproot from their stakes and go tumbling end over end across the tundra toward the mountain. We stayed at the campground for an hour and then had to get back on the bus for the trip back. It was just as amazing to see everything in reverse. The lighting was different, and it made the mountain sparkle in the sunlight. The ride into Denali Park to see Mt. McKinley was long, bumpy, and dusty, but worth every minute of every bit of bad weather we encountered to get here.

The next day was a day to rest, do laundry, and get prepared for the final few days of the trip. Tim decided he'd go hiking alone and came back with bloody knees, elbows, and hips from a fall down a rock-covered slope. Between the stitches he got in Canada from his bike wreck, and the scrapes he got in Denali Park, he'd have some interesting memories to tell his grandkids. At sunset, we were treated to a light show by the fading sunlight playing off the clouds and mountains. We went to bed happy.

23

August 6–9

◆

3,231 miles from Missoula

I enjoyed the next day's ride even though it was into a fierce headwind for most of the morning. Intermittent showers plagued us in the afternoon. We saw some beautiful country and crossed Broad Pass at an elevation of 2,300 feet. The road over the pass was so gradual that we weren't sure when we reached the top. After fifty-one miles, we pulled in to the East Fork rest area for the night. Dinner was very relaxed with a lot of joking and banter. The weather was threatening again, so we set our tents up under the roof of the rest area picnic shelter. Strange looking, perhaps, but effective at keeping our tents dry. Three more riding days! I was elated and sad at the same time. It seemed as if the first few days of the trip would never end, and now the days were flying past much too quickly. We were all looking forward to ending the trip in Anchorage. At the same time, we were sorry to see it end.

Rain, rain, rain! All day. No substitutes. It poured, hard, for about two hours and made the morning very wet. Inexplicably, it was my best day of riding for the whole trip. There was a terrific tailwind that pushed us along, and we rode incredibly fast. The road was flat and we rode seventy miles in 4 1/2 hours, mostly in our highest gears. When we got to Trapper's Creek, there was a store, café, and laundry. We washed and dried our clothes and took showers. It was still raining and cold outside, so we stayed inside the café the rest of the day. It stopped raining long enough for us to eat dinner and to put up the tents. I was hoping the rain would stop; my hair looked good dry.

The next day I just couldn't seem to get going. It was the direct opposite of the ride the day before when everything clicked. I was slow getting out of camp, clunky on the ride, and so tired that I had to take an hours rest break at lunch.

The juices just weren't flowing. The milestones of the day were that John had his thirteenth flat tire, Garry broke three spokes, and I ate five sandwiches for lunch.

We decided to ride another fifteen miles to Wasilla in hopes of finding a good campground for the last night. We lucked out and found a nice campground with shelters next to a lake. Just in time, too-it started raining. The total mileage of the day was seventy-three. We had about thirty-two miles to Anchorage on the last day.

I spent the day reflecting on the trip now that we were near the end. And I couldn't believe we were near the end. I chuckled at my testosterone-driven arrogance about my bike riding abilities. I ruefully remembered the painfully exhilarating ride over Going to the Sun Highway and the subsequent knee problems. I remembered the inventor guy that picked me up in B.C.; the afternoon and night in Canal Flats dodging loggers looking for a party; looking eye-to-eye with a baby moose outside of Lake Louise; riding with the Indian family; Mary inviting me to join them; running back and forth to the outhouse during a long night when I was sick in Smithers; blowing my cool on the ride to Stewart; appreciating the kindness of the vicar, Sheila; spending the long, bumpy days on gravel; seeing the woman swatting bugs at a rest area; catching animals like the wolf and bears by surprise next to the road; the Watson Lake signposts; the quiet of the Yukon; the best swimming hole in history at the Lapie River Campground; True Grizz hill and the hills we named for the three bears; the Klondike Gold Rush and everything in Dawson City; the epic ride across the Top of the World Highway; the last climb into Alaska; the beer-swilling horse at the Richardson Roadhouse; the three milkshakes in less than ten minutes in Fairbanks; the first look at Mt. McKinley from over 100 miles away; the bus trip into Denali Park; and the ride in the rain where everything clicked.

After spending so much time with these guys, I figured it would be hard to say goodbye knowing I might never see any of them again. We had had an experience of a lifetime in a little over two months. We shared rain, snow, dust, gravel, long days in the saddle, and food. We drank from streams, pooped in the woods, and skinny-dipped whenever possible. We battled mosquitoes, blackflies, deerflies, and each other. I got to know some of the guys really well, and some preferred to stay distant, even to the end.

I felt a great sense of accomplishment as we were about to ride into Anchorage the next day. I had battled through my own unpreparedness, knee problems, and questions about whether to stay on the trip, especially after Tom, Pete, and Steve left. I had been sick, and kept going, I had gone nutso on the way to Stewart, and kept going. I could put up or take down my tent in a driving rain in less than five minutes. I could make a dinner for seven, on a one burner Coleman stove, with little more than potatoes, and some assorted vegetables and eggs. I could fix my tires, clean my chain, and repair my freewheel while standing beside a dirt road. I could ride day after day over some of the worst gravel roads in North America and be ready for more the next morning. I had seen some of the most astonishing and awe-inspiring scenery imaginable. And I had been to the mountain, Mt. McKinley.

WE MADE IT! We cruised the last thirty-two miles into Anchorage on August 9. We rode into town like we owned the place. It was unbelievably satisfying to ride through the city all together. We were wet and looked like we had ridden from Montana. Our jackets and pants had faded, our hair was blonder. Our faces had that ruddy outdoors look. I'm sure our eyes were brighter and our step bouncier than when we started. Garry led us on a victory lap around downtown to our end-of-ride luncheon at McDonalds, the first we had seen since Montana. It had been rainy and about 53F while we were riding. It was just a typical day for us. After lunch, we all went to the overlook at Captain Cook's Inlet for our end-of-trip picture.

We had started as ten anxious riders and finished as seven grizzled bikers. Our numbers said it all: The total trip, one way, was about 3,300 miles, with about 1,300 miles of that on gravel. We had some sort of inclement weather fifty-four out of sixty-seven days. The highest temperature was in the 80's in Yukon and the lowest was 23F at Denali National Park. We wore out twenty-two tires and had thirty flats among the seven of us, and also had sixteen broken spokes, one broken rear axle, two broken freewheels, one cracked rear hub, and several broken pannier racks. Garry was the leader with nine broken spokes and John had thirteen flats to his credit. Tim had the most mishaps with his tumble over his handlebars in B.C. and his tumble down the hill in Denali. And Henry made the most friends.

Tim and I flew from Anchorage to Missoula to pick up my car for the trip home. Tim went to Tennessee with me for a few days and then took a plane home to Milwaukee. Arnold, John, and Henry, rode back through eastern Alaska to catch the ferry home. Dale planned to enroll in dental school. Garry stayed in Anchorage.

Epilogue

As I write this, some twenty-four years after our trip, I am married with two great kids. Dale has retired as a dentist and works for fun part-time for his local police department; Garry still lives in Anchorage and has worked in a number of businesses and internet ventures; Arnold is married with two boys and owns a construction company; Tim is a stay-at-home dad with his daughter; John, a cross country truck driver, is married with a couple of step grandkids; Sadly, Henry died in 2000. According to his son, he continued riding and took another trip across the U.S. by bicycle in his late sixties.

Notes and Acknowledgments

The story you've read is accurate as far as my memory and journal from the trip are concerned. It is impossible to remember conversations verbatim after 24 years, but I've tried to represent the thoughts, feelings, and emotions of the time.

Students of geography may quibble with some of my mileages. The mileages came from the itinerary sent by the tour leader, Garry, before the trip. They are accurate as much as possible in a time before odometers for bicycles were widely available. If you still have issue, ride it yourself.

I've wanted to write a book about my trip for a long time, but could never quite find the time. I want to thank my wife, Leslie, for incenting me with a $200 bribe, and the promise of a party upon completion of the book. I also want to thank my kids, Will and Nelle, for their willingness to read chapters and make comments and suggestions.

My friend, May Lamar Donnell, an author herself, gave me a lot of encouragement, and said, "The best way to write a book is just to sit down and start writing." She has also patiently answered questions about publishing with a publisher and self-publishing.

Susan Hawkins Harris sent me a book about writing books. Jennifer Parada Wheeler provided friendship and motivation.

Joe Johnson for his technical bicycle knowledge.

Two professor friends from Davidson College, Tony Abbott and Earl Edmondson, agreed to be my readers, with the understanding that this is not an attempt at scholarly writing, and that it has been twenty-four years since anyone graded one of my papers.

Tony, an English professor, and award winning author, read the story for flow and continuity. History professor and author, Earl, read the story for grammar and syntax, both of which took me about a week of late nights to correct. I am indebted to them both, and appreciate their friendship and willingness to look at the story during their summer vacations.

978-0-595-37350-5
0-595-37350-X

Printed in the United Kingdom by
Lightning Source UK Ltd., Milton Keynes
140613UK00002BA/34/A